IS YOUR MIND YOUR FRIEND?

12 PRINCIPLES FOR CLARITY OF THOUGHT AND PEACE OF MIND

TARUN GULATI

"Contemplation is the Mother of Clarity."

"If you live your life largely looking outward and not inward, then you aren't deeply connected with yourself, so you lack internal clarity, so you may tend to make choices that seem exciting in the short run but may not be right for your long-term peace of mind. This leads to stress, anxiety and restlessness. "

"The solution is to spend some time in Contemplation, alone, in silence, on the Adios principles. This helps you think more clearly, so you can find the answers that are right for you, without depending on anyone else, for the rest of your life. If you train your inner counselor, you will never need to depend on an external one."

This book is dedicated to clarity of thought and peace of mind.

CONTENTS

PART ONE: INTRODUCTION

1. HOW TO MAKE THE RIGHT CHOICES?

YOUR GOAL IS NOT the pursuit of happiness. It is the pursuit of peace of mind. The method to get there is Contemplation.

As you go through various phases of your life, you might play multiple roles over the years - you might be a student, friend, partner, team member, business owner, leader, parent, child, believer, creator, and many more. In each of these roles, you might need to make decisions. In some of these roles, your decisions might be so important that they could shape the very quality of your life.

The quality of your life depends on how you feel. If you feel good, the quality of your life is good. If you don't feel good, the quality of your life is not so good. The question then is, how would you like to feel? If you want to feel fulfilled, purposeful and peaceful, you need to make choices that can help you feel that way. To make those choices, there are two prerequisites:

1. You need to be deeply connected with yourself, so you know yourself very well; and
2. You need your own personal, customized method or system that can help you make those right choices.

3

Since these choices are about your life, if you don't know yourself deeply, how will you know what is good for you, what makes you fulfilled and peaceful? You may know what you want, but what you want may not necessarily be good for your long-term fulfillment or peace of mind. Hence, a deep connection with yourself is necessary. But that is not sufficient.

You also need a personal method or system that helps you make the right choices - choices that are right for you specifically, even though they may not be right for someone else. This personal method helps you choose between various alternatives - should I do this or that - and select the one that will make you most fulfilled and peaceful.

Also, only having a deep connection without a system that tells you how to make the right choice is not sufficient because without that system, your inner connection might only amplify the wrong voice inside of you and get you to make the wrong decision. Again. Unless you have a filter that specifically says, - Does this choice make me more peaceful, or will it take away my peace of mind? - the process isn't complete.

So, to make the right choices, the two prerequisites are:

- a deep connection with yourself, and
- a personal system that helps you make the right choices.

BUT WHAT COULD BE THE PROBLEM?

The problem is that we live in a world that is extremely noisy and distracting, a world that is scientifically designed to keep your attention outside most of the time. If you live your life largely looking outward and not looking inward, you may not be able to create a deep connection with yourself. If you are not deeply connected with yourself, you may not have created your personal system or method to make the right choices, not because you cannot create it, but because you have been too busy looking outward. You might be paying too much attention to what is happening in the external world - what others are doing, saying, etc. - rather than looking inward and having a regular dialogue with yourself on what would make your life fulfilling, purposeful and peaceful.

If you live your life largely focused on the outside, you might tend to make choices that seem exciting in the short run but are not right for you in the long run. You may make your choices based on impulse, emotion, or imitation. They may make you feel good in the moment but diminish your long-term peace of mind. You may say something to someone that you shouldn't just because you react emotionally. You may do something just because many others around you are doing it, without asking if it will make you feel peaceful in the long run. You may make wrong decisions about your partner, work, children or other important aspects in your life.

If you live largely looking outward, you can create an exciting life, an adventurous life, a wealthy life, a famous life, perhaps. But a fulfilling, purposeful and peaceful life? Difficult. Since the world is designed to pull and keep your attention outside constantly, you need to invest specific energy and effort to counter that and turn your attention inward. You need a method that will train you to stop focusing outward, turn inward and create a deep connection with yourself.

That method is Contemplation.

A regular habit of Contemplation will help you achieve the first prerequisite for making the right choices - a deep connection with yourself.

To achieve the second prerequisite - a personal method and system to make the right choices - this book will provide you with a few principles using which you will be able to construct your own personal system of making choices that are right for you. This system is personal, very specific to you because you will construct it using the priorities, phase and architecture of your own life. Your system can be very different from mine, or your best friend's system, or the system of someone successful that you admire, even though all of us are using the same underlying principles. This is because the choices that you make will be very specific to your life, and only you know how something makes you feel. Only you can decide whether something makes you more peaceful or less peaceful. No one else can.

Not only might your choices be different from other people, but they might also be different from your own choices depending upon your phase of life. Even within your own system, you might make a particular choice today, but at another time in your life, for the same situation, you might make a very different choice because your phase of life might have changed, your circumstances might be different. That is why it is important to have your own personal, customized system that works for your life specifically.

If you train your inner counselor, you may never need to depend on an external one. Using these two tools - Contemplation and your personal method of making choices - you can find the answers to any questions that might arise in your life. These questions could be mundane - should I do the laundry, should we buy this television, what should I wear, what music should I listen to, or they could be profound - what is my life's vision, how should I do meaningful work, should I be in a relationship, should I have kids, how should I raise my child well, etc.

Contemplation of these principles will help you find your answers to many important questions in your life.

A regular habit of Contemplation will help you create and maintain a deep connection with yourself, and the principles will help you create your personal system of making the right choices -

your own decision-making framework - that you
dimension of your life, for the rest of your life.

To recap, the quality of your life depends on how y
wish to feel fulfilled, purposeful and peaceful, you
choices that make you feel that way. To make the right choices,
you need a deep connection with yourself and a system to make
the right choice in each situation. Contemplation helps you
create a deep connection with yourself, and the principles will
help you create your own system to make the right choices.
Make the right choices, and you will create a fulfilled, purposeful, and peaceful life.

WHY DO YOU NEED A PERSONAL DECISION-MAKING FRAMEWORK?

A personal system or framework helps you think through
matters in a systematic manner and make the decisions that are
right for you in the long term. Without such a system, you might
make decisions impulsively or based on an untrained instinct,
sometimes merely based on what feels good at the moment, or at
other times by getting unduly influenced by someone else or by
imitating others just because many people seem to be doing a
particular thing.

Making impulsive decisions without thinking through well
could be considered normal today. But merely because it is
normal - merely because many people do it that way, does not
necessarily mean that it is the right way to do it. A unanimous
decision is just that - a unanimous decision. It is not necessarily a
correct decision. Just because everyone has agreed on something
does not necessarily mean that they have agreed on the right
thing.

To make decisions that are right for you, you need your own,
customized decision-making framework that contains your

rsonal set of lenses through which you can examine every decision - personal or professional - and make only those decisions that are right for you in that phase in life. They may not be right for someone else, but that does not matter. Your colleague, neighbor or friend may not agree with you. But the question is, have you thought through it well, using your own framework? Your decision must be right for you because the outcome will affect your peace of mind, not someone else's. That is what matters.

'What should I do in this scenario' is a very important question, the answer to which can sometimes change the course of your life dramatically. If you choose a wrong partner, behave wrongly with the right partner, choose the wrong work or organization, maintain a wrong attitude about your work, choose to live in the wrong place, fail to create a healthy environment for your kids, surround yourself with wrong friends or colleagues, you may never get to live a fulfilled, purposeful, and peaceful life. That is true for a very large number of people in the world today.

That is why it is important that you have your own, personalized decision-making system that helps you think clearly in each scenario, so you make the right choices. In all the above scenarios and many more, you need to make decisions on a regular basis. If you don't have your own inner compass clearly guiding you, you might tend to make decisions in a hurry or be influenced by what your friend or colleague is doing in that situation. You may not consider whether it is good for your own fulfillment and long-term peace of mind. Having your own system keeps you on the right track.

The method outlined in this book will help you create that personalized decision-making system for yourself. That method is called ADIOS - A Dialogue In Objective Silence, because that is what it is. It is a dialogue that you have with yourself, objectively, in silence.

The ADIOS framework combines the skill of Contemplation and certain Adios principles to help you create a personalized decision-making system for yourself. By following the ADIOS method, you will improve your clarity of thought and make such choices that leave you more peaceful. Having a clear mind isn't enough. A violent husband, a cheating wife, an unethical businessman or a toxic boss might also possess extreme clarity in their mind as to what they are about to do. But the quality of that clarity should be such that it leads to a more peaceful mind. If you fail that test, if your clarity leads to you becoming more restless or less peaceful eventually, that is the wrong kind of clarity of thought.

ADIOS has 'peace of mind' as the ultimate objective of all decisions you make. So, you find solutions or answers to critical situations or questions in your life by practicing regular Contemplation on the ADIOS principles, but those solutions or answers must be such that make you more peaceful. As you think through your questions, you use the ADIOS principles as your personalized system of making the right choices and based on what makes you more or less peaceful, you might sometimes decide to change your actions or thoughts to make them more aligned with your overall inner peace. Once you practice and apply the principles for a few days and make your choices accordingly, at home and outside, you start to notice a conspicuous feeling of lasting peace inside of you.

Peace of mind is a skill, just like riding a bicycle or playing a musical instrument - you can learn it by using certain principles and practicing them for some time. Adios teaches you, slowly, step by step, how to understand your thoughts, observe the resulting actions, and notice the impact of those thoughts and actions on your peace of mind.

Once you have understood the Adios principles and acquired a habit of Contemplation to think deeply about them, you have learned the skill of keeping your mind peaceful. Remember, peace of mind is a skill that you can learn and improve with practice. You first understand the principles that help you think more clearly and in a manner that leads to a more peaceful mind, and then you apply them to your daily life. Contemplation is the tool you use to engrave these principles on your mind, and to analyze important life situations or find answers and insights you are looking for in a particular situation, personal or professional. So, while this will help you find answers to your personal questions, it will also help you get better at the work you do.

By consistently applying the Adios method for a few weeks, you will slowly build your own set of personal lenses through which you can look at any, and I mean any, situation in life, and be absolutely clear as to what you are supposed to do, and not supposed to do, and why. You will construct your own personal moral compass that will guide you at various junctures on your journey. In many instances, you will have your answer even before you have asked your question - a very powerful mental state to be in. This will happen for sure. Very naturally. It is just a matter of time and some practice.

ROLES IN LIFE

You would need to make decisions in many roles you might play in your life. Some decisions could define the very direction your life might take in the future, while others might not be so profound but still be important.

Student

As a student, there are many decisions you will have to make, from choosing your academic focus to deciding where to study and which institution to attend. With so many options available, it can be challenging to know where to start.

You may need to consider various factors, such as the quality of education offered, the reputation of the institution, the location and cost of living, and the potential career opportunities available in your chosen field. Once you have chosen your course of study and institution, you will need to make decisions about how to prioritize your time and focus on developing skills and experiences that will help you achieve your career goals.

After studying, you may need to decide whether to pursue further education or enter the workforce. If you choose the latter, you will have to consider which organizations and roles best align with your interests and qualifications. This may involve researching companies, networking with professionals in your field, and weighing various factors such as salary, location, and company culture.

As a student, it is normal to feel overwhelmed by these decisions, but by using Contemplation on the Adios principles and adequate research in the respective matter, you can make informed choices that not only set you up for success in your academic and professional life, but also ensure that you live a fulfilling, meaningful and peaceful life. A fairly high number of people choose to study or work in a domain that is not right for them and pay for this dearly through lack of fulfillment most of their life. Contemplation will help you avoid making such mistakes.

Business Leader

As a business leader, one major concern may be deciding on the right product or service to offer and developing a strategy to bring it to the market successfully. The skill of Contemplation enables you to think deeply and find hidden insights. It will help you look closely at what you do, identify your key strengths, and understand the uniqueness of your business so you can differentiate and position yourself in a noisy, competitive market.

It is very tempting to do what many others are doing, in a manner that many others are doing, but that may not add any real value to the customer. After many months of consistent but mindless busyness, you might realize that you don't really have anything unique or even useful, and that might lead to an uncomfortable feeling of hollowness within - What am I really doing? How will we survive if we have nothing useful to offer? Contemplation and the Adios principles will help you find the right answers to these and many other questions.

You may have concerns related to hiring and retaining the right team members, particularly if you are operating with limited resources. This may require you to consider your company culture, values, and vision, and to create an inspiring workplace that attracts and retains top talent. A leader passionate about their non-financial vision has a much better probability of attracting and retaining the right people. Contemplation will not only help you gain clarity about your values and purpose but also provide you with the conviction you need to present them to your current and future employees and partners.

You may need to raise financial resources to support your business, such as securing funding from investors or bank loans. A deep connection with yourself will help you choose the right financial partners, rather than rushing into that decision and choosing someone who might look more attractive today but may not be aligned with your values and vision. If you don't feel energized and feel that you are strongly aligned when you speak with them, you should think twice before saying yes. Contemplation will help you slow down, go deep within, and understand how you really feel about the partnership, so you don't make a wrong choice. A wrong investor could change everything. The same goes for the right investor. In some cases, you might even settle for a lower valuation because you see a better match in terms of values and non-financial vision. The Adios principles will ensure you don't make such decisions in a hurry.

You may need to develop an appropriate product and marketing strategy. Using Contemplation strategically, you can find the voice for your product that your sales and marketing strategy can follow. Your go-to-market strategy can also be very specific to your own long-term vision. In a noisy world, it is tempting and easier to follow what someone else is doing. But if you don't find your own unique voice, it will come back to bite you, eventually. Contemplation will help you find your uniqueness. It will help you unlock your you.

If this sounds too simplistic and theoretical, ask yourself - how much time do you and your leadership team spend each week doing nothing but only thinking deeply about the uniqueness of your business? If you don't put in the effort, do not expect a result.

Partner

As a partner in a relationship, there may be several decisions to make. The first is deciding on the right person to be your partner, and then developing a strong and healthy relationship with them.

You must identify your personal values and priorities and find someone who shares them. If you choose someone based on superficial factors or to quickly fill a void in your life, the relationship may bring more misery than joy. Before you find your partner, you must find yourself. If you don't know who you are, what you really want, and who you want it with, you might choose the wrong person. Multiple times. Contemplation of the Adios principles will help you think about what would make you feel fulfilled and peaceful in a relationship, what kind of partner might enhance or reduce your peace of mind and what you really value in that relationship.

Once you are in a relationship, maintaining a fulfilling and happy relationship will also require some thought and energy.

Choices must be made each day in terms of what to say, do and what not to. Contemplation will help you make the right choices. The Adios principles will help you keep your cool in challenging situations, which might be important to maintain the relationship in the long term. Internal clarity helps you focus on what really matters - care, love, attention and respect - to maintain the warmth in your relationship.

Parent

As a parent, you may have concerns about various aspects of your child's life. You might want them to grow up with the right values so they can live a peaceful life. It's natural to feel concerned if your child displays worrisome behaviors like aggression or unnecessary rebellion. You might be concerned about them falling into bad company. This could be due to what they see at home, the kind of friends they have at school or the type of online activities they engage in. Unless you possess clarity of thought about your values and the kind of environment you wish to give your child, such problems are difficult to handle and, if not handled well at the right time, can have long-term negative consequences.

Many parents struggle with finding the right balance between work and family life. You may worry that you're not spending enough quality time with your children. This is quite common, especially in larger cities where people struggle to balance their stressful jobs with their family responsibilities. Contemplation will help you find that right balance. You might also tend to negatively compare yourself with other parents or your child with other children and feel bad about their upbringing. The Adios principles will help you think through such issues clearly and find the right answers.

Effective communication with your children is crucial, and it's common to have concerns about it. You might worry about understanding their needs or expressing your thoughts and feelings in a way they can comprehend and connect with. There could be issues around growing irritability or aggression in their communication. This can also be very relevant and sensitive depending upon the age of the child. The Adios principles will help you think clearly in such situations and apply them in your daily life when you speak to your kids, partner and others at home, so you maintain the right environment for your kids.

Doubts about your parenting style can also arise often. You may question whether you're being too strict or too lenient. You and your partner might have very different backgrounds and hence different parenting styles that you might need to balance. Trying to always project your approach as the best may not be the best way to deal with such situations. Contemplation will help you remain calm and think deeply about the right solution so you can continue to maintain a healthy relationship with your partner as well as your child. Questions such as 'Am I being a good parent?' or 'Are we meeting our child's emotional and physical needs in the best way possible?' can also come up frequently. Your internal clarity of thought is very important in such scenarios. The Adios principles will ensure that you focus on looking inward to find your answers rather than getting unduly influenced by the external world while making your choices.

By practicing Contemplation on the Adios principles, you will also be motivated to personally embody the qualities of calmness and peace of mind so you can create the right environment for your child. A child learns a lot from what is happening around them. They are significantly influenced by the way their parents behave on a regular basis at home. Living a life that feels fulfilling, purposeful and peaceful is the best way to enable your child to set up a peaceful life for themselves. You can't do it for them, no matter how badly you wish you could. Only they can do it, with their own mind. So then what can you do as a parent? How can you help?

If they are going to define their life using their own mind, you can help by training their mind in the right direction by creating an environment of self-reflection, prioritizing long-term peace of mind over short-term excitement and by demonstrating these qualities by living them yourself. If they watch you use profanity regularly, but you give them a dead moral stare saying "Language!" when they use a bad word, that isn't going to help. You will lack credibility in their eyes, whether they tell you this or not. You need to lead the way through your actions.

Respect cannot be demanded. It must be earned through your actions. Contemplation will help you do that.

Life is, in essence, feeling. How you feel determines the quality of your life. How you feel depends largely upon what you do, say, and think. If you aren't deeply connected with yourself and don't know what really makes you fulfilled and peaceful, you might make the wrong decisions. If you make wrong decisions in the roles you play in your life, you may not feel very peaceful.

WHY MUST CONTEMPLATION BE THE BASIS OF YOUR DECISIONS?

Our ultimate objective is to live a fulfilling, purposeful, and peaceful life. To do that, you must be deeply connected with yourself. The world might encourage you to mostly look outward and not inward, because of which you might lose touch with yourself. If you are not connected with yourself on a regular basis, creating a fulfilling and peaceful life is quite difficult. Contemplation helps you create and maintain that connection with yourself, so you can create a life that is worthwhile.

Life entails a series of decisions almost every day. Hence, the quality of your life - peaceful or restless, fulfilling or wanting, meaningful or shallow - will also depend on the quality of these decisions you make daily.

If you make decisions using a distracted mind, one that mostly looks outward into the world, is restless and lacks clarity, your decisions will most likely not be right for you - they will not lead to long-term peace of mind. The world continues to present more and more avenues to distract you and keep your attention outside. Contemplation is the method to safeguard yourself from this continuous onslaught of distraction and restlessness. The Adios principles will help you make decisions that make you more peaceful, the ones that are right for you.

What you see many people around you do quite often may not necessarily be right for you. It might be right for them, but not for you. Sometimes, it is not even right for them, but they do it anyway because they haven't thought about it deeply.

You must.

Focus on the inside before you take a plunge into the outside. Let Contemplation be the basis for all your decisions that matter.

What could go wrong if you make wrong decisions? A lot. As you read through these examples, think about whether they apply to your life or someone you care about.

John stood at the edge of the cliff, watching the waves crash against the rocks far below. He was a student, just out of college, and he had made some wrong choices in his life.

He had always been a bright student, with a head full of ideas and a heart full of dreams. But when it came time to choose a stream of study, he was unsure. John had looked at the various options, but nothing had really resonated with him. In the end, he had chosen a course in business management, thinking it was the safe and sensible option.

But as he sat through his classes, he felt increasingly bored and uninterested. He found himself daydreaming about other things, about the adventures he could be having if he wasn't stuck in a classroom. He started skipping classes, and soon enough, he had fallen behind in his studies.

As graduation approached, John began to panic. He didn't know what he wanted to do after college, and he felt like he had wasted his time and money on a degree that he didn't care about. He started frantically searching for jobs, sending out countless resumes and attending job fairs. But nothing seemed to fit.

Eventually, he took a job at a small company in a city he didn't know much about. He hoped that it would be a fresh start, a chance to reinvent himself and find his place in the world. But he quickly realized that he had made another mistake. The job was boring and unfulfilling, and he struggled to make friends in a new place.

As the weeks turned into months, John began to feel trapped. He had made so many wrong choices, and he didn't know how to get back on track. He felt like he was standing at the edge of a cliff, with nowhere to go.

John looked down at the waves below, and for a moment, he thought about jumping. But then he closed his eyes and took a deep breath. He knew that he couldn't keep making the wrong choices forever. It was time to find clarity.

He opened his eyes and turned away from the edge of the cliff. He didn't know where his path would lead him, but he knew that he had to start somewhere.

Joan's passion for graphic design had always driven her. She knew that starting her own business would not be an easy task. Despite this, she was ready to take on the challenges and make her dream a reality.

As she started her business, Joan quickly realized that she had a lot to learn.

"What sets me apart from other graphic designers?" Joan pondered.

"How can I position myself to attract the clients I want to work with?"

Her thoughts were interrupted by the sound of her phone ringing. It was a potential client who had found her website online. Joan was excited but nervous. She knew this was her chance to prove her worth as a professional graphic designer.

During the phone call, the client asked about Joan's experience and pricing. Joan spoke too much, way too fast, stumbled over her words and ultimately failed to communicate her value clearly. She sounded desperate. It happened again the next day, and the next. The clients were hesitant, and Joan could sense it. Something was clearly missing. She had to figure this out.

Paul was passionate about his business idea and was determined to bring it to life. He knew exactly what he wanted to create, and he had assembled a team of talented individuals to help him meet his goals. However, he soon realized that his hiring process had been a significant mistake.

Paul's mistake was clear, and he voiced it to his mentor, "I have realized that I have made a mistake in the hiring process. I hired people too quickly only on the basis of their intelligence and where they had worked earlier, but some of them did not share our vision and values. This has created an unhealthy culture where making money has now become the primary purpose. The employees have become transactional in their conversations, sometimes even hostile enough to threaten resignation if their unreasonable financial needs are not met. We are clearly headed for a disaster."

His mentor nodded in agreement, and Paul knew that he had to make changes if his business was to succeed. He had to focus on hiring people who shared his passion and values, even if they were less experienced than other candidates in certain roles.

Paul knew this was important if he had to create an inspiring institution that his team members would be proud to be a part of.

Emily and her partner Steve had been together for over a year when Steve started to notice a concerning pattern in her behavior. Emily loved to party and drink, often to excess, which led to her neglecting her responsibilities and commitments. Steve tried to talk to her about it, expressing his concerns and hopes for their future, but Emily always dismissed his worries and replied, "I'm still young. I need to live a little! I'll get to work and responsibilities later. Right now, I just want to have fun!"

As time went on, Steve found himself increasingly frustrated with her behavior. He loved her and wanted to build a future with her, but he knew that her wild lifestyle would not be conducive to a healthy and responsible relationship, let alone raising a child together.

"Emily, I'm worried about you," he said to her one day. "I love you, but I can't keep watching you neglect your responsibilities and commitments. It's not fair to me, and it's not fair to yourself."

Emily listened, but she didn't take his words seriously. She continued staying out late regularly and drinking excessively, even when it started to negatively affect their relationship.

Eventually, Steve was exhausted. He had tried enough, but he knew that he couldn't continue to be with someone who didn't share his values and wasn't willing to make changes for the better.

"I'm sorry, Emily," he said as he ended the relationship. "I care about you, but I can't be with someone who doesn't take responsibility for their actions and neglects their commitments. It seems your personal lifestyle is more important to you than our relationship so I think I should leave you to it. I wish you love and luck, but it is best that we go our separate ways."

Emily was heartbroken. She couldn't believe what had just happened. She was devastated, but deep down, she knew that her partner was right.

If you lack internal clarity and do now know what will make you feel more fulfilled, what will make your work meaningful and what will make you more peaceful, then you might make wrong decisions in your personal and professional life.

HOW CAN ADIOS HELP YOU?

ADIOS stands for A Dialogue In Objective Silence. It is a dialogue that you have with yourself, objectively, in silence. When you train yourself in Contemplation on the Adios principles, you are essentially training yourself to become closer to yourself. You are taking a journey back to yourself, a journey you perhaps forgot to take because you were too busy with the outside world. You must be one with yourself on the inside so you can make the right decisions on the outside.

The Adios method trains you to think deeply about matters that matter to you. You analyze them and try finding answers to your questions by thinking deeply about the Adios principles.

The Adios framework is based on peace of mind as the objective. You practice making such decisions that lead to a more peaceful state of mind, not decisions that provide short-term excitement, advantage or pleasure. When you train yourself in this manner for a period of time, you develop the skill to find answers to all your questions on your own, without relying on anyone else, and you know which answers are right for you and the ones that are not.

The Adios approach is - if you train your inner counselor, you will never need to depend on an external one. Contemplation on the Adios principles will help you do that. You will learn these principles in the chapters that follow.

There are two primary problems today:

1. People are more restless and distracted. They are spending much more time looking outward and very little time looking inward.

2. Many people do not have a well-defined, written down set of internal guidelines to refer to before making a personal or professional decision.

Combine the two, and you get:

- someone who is trying to make decisions almost daily
- but with a restless mind, mostly looking outward, and
- does not have an internal reference point to draw the right guidance from.

This leads to you making some wrong choices based on looking at what others are doing (who themselves may not be very clear and peaceful), or on the basis of impulse, emotion or short-term satisfaction rather than what will make you peaceful in the long run. This eventually leads to an agitated mind, and sometimes stress, anxiety or worse.

We do not have a mental health problem in the world. We have a mental clarity problem.

Other than those who might have a medical condition and need clinical intervention, for most other people, confusion, anxiety, and an uneasy mind are the result of a lack of clarity. Most people are not unwell. They are unclear. Most modern stress is due to the two problems mentioned above.

That is actually a good thing. Because the solution then is not as hard as it is made out to be. Clarity of thought and peace of mind are skills that can be learned, much like playing a musical instrument or riding a bicycle. You don't have to be gifted. You don't have to be a genius. You can learn them, practice them, and master them and create a fulfilling, purposeful and peaceful life for yourself.

This book will show you how.

As you read, please work with me. Please break down your thoughts and actions you might carry out during your day, analyze them, and think about them for a few minutes each day. Think about specific questions or situations in your life that are important that you want to find an answer to or resolve. You will learn certain principles and tools that will enable you to think more clearly and create a more peaceful state of mind. As you read this book, use these principles to find answers to the questions or situations in your life.

We will use the Adios framework to do this. Adios stands for A Dialogue In Objective Silence. It is a system that trains you:

i. To improve your clarity of thought,

ii. Using that clarity of thought, make such decisions that lead to a more peaceful state of mind, and

iii. To be able to do this on your own, independently, without relying on anyone else, forever.

If you train your inner counselor, you will never need to depend on an external one. This book will show you how to become completely independent in making your own decisions. You can take inputs and guidance from others when needed, but you will train yourself to take all that external information and use Contemplation on the Adios principles to find your own answer, the answer that is right for you, in your current phase of life.

These could be questions relating to your education, work, relationships, parenting, self-growth, finances, retirement, or any other dimension in your life. The questions could be mundane or profound. The goal is to enable you to find all the answers, on your own, forever. And only such answers that will make your life more peaceful, not more restless, in the long run overall.

I say "overall" because certain actions might reduce your peace of mind in the short run to achieve larger peace of mind in the long run. You will make these decisions on your own, including deciding whether you wish to sacrifice your peace of mind in the short term to gain a much longer-term peace of mind.

I will not provide you with any answers to your specific life situations, because I cannot. No one really can. It is your life, only you will live it and feel it, so only you must find that right answer – the answer that is right for you. This book will instead train you to think deeply so you can make the decisions that you believe are right for you, and make those decisions on your own, independently, without relying on anyone else, forever. And also take responsibility for the consequences of those decisions.

This is not difficult. It might take a few days of practice, but it is not difficult. Commit to practicing the Adios system for 10 minutes each day, for at least three days a week. If you do that, you will start to see a conspicuous difference in about three weeks.

I have personally practiced, experimented with, and experienced the tools in this book for more than 15,000 hours over the last 15 years consciously, and subconsciously for over 25 years. The Adios principles you will learn come from my endless hours of thinking deeply, observing my own actions and what impact they have on my peace of mind, observing others, making changes in my behavior to test whether it improves my peace of mind, and training countless other people. It is an ongoing process that continues every day. As I try these experiments, and many more, I make my own customizations. You will too. That is the goal. You need to take these tools and make them your own.

It is your life. It is your decision.

Never believe. Not me. Not anyone else. Try it yourself and see if it helps you.

Experiment. Experience. Evaluate.

Resolve to work with yourself for about ten minutes a day each day. Resolve to create a deeper connection with yourself, a connection that will stay forever. Resolve to become your best friend, forever.

I suggest you read this book in the following manner. If you wish, read it cover to cover once so you understand what it is about. Then read it again, but this time, read it very slowly, deliberately, over a few weeks, focusing on specific chapters each week and practicing those principles. If you prefer a more guided and systematic approach, you can read it while also going through the online Adios Contemplation Program on www.adiosworld.com.

For the next few days, I propose a division of labor. I will focus on training you. You focus on practicing what we discuss for 10 mins each day. I will be true to my word. You be true to yours.

Let us begin.

CHAPTER TAKEAWAYS:

- Your goal is not the pursuit of happiness. It is the pursuit of peace of mind. Contemplation of the Adios principles is the method to get there.
- You need your own personal decision-making system so you can make decisions that are right for you, that make you feel more fulfilled and peaceful.

- Adios principles help you create your own personal decision-making system.
- Without Contemplation, you may tend to focus outward and make decisions based on external influence. These decisions may not be right for you.
- You need to make critical decisions in various dimensions of your life - education, relationship, parenting, work. Use the Adios principles to make the right decisions.
- Experiment, experience and evaluate. Try Contemplation on the Adios principles yourself and assess what impact it has on your peace of mind.

~

2. CLARITY AND PEACE

Let us be clear about what we are trying to do. Recall the two primary problems:

1. People are more restless and distracted. They are spending much more time looking outward and very little time looking inward.

2. Many people do not have a well-defined, written down set of internal guidelines - a personal decision-making system - to refer to before making a personal or professional decision.

This process of decision-making, where you focus mostly on the outside and very little on the inside, leads to you making choices that may not necessarily be right for you. Because you are not deeply connected with yourself, you might tend to make your choices by imitating others. What others do influences you a lot more if you lack internal clarity. Your internal voice is missing, but you still need to make a decision, and you are looking outside most of the time. So, the only influence you have is external.

You might look at a successful business leader and think – I should be doing that too. You might look at another parent and say, – I should do what she does for her child. You might look at your boss who always carries a serious and angry attitude and think – That is what being professional means so I should be like him. You might look at your classmate many years later and think - they are more successful than I am, so I am a failure. You might look at someone else's partner and say – Mine should be like them.

Maybe you are right. But maybe you are not, and you are only getting unduly influenced by the external environment. It helps to be sure as to what you really want, and also to be sure what you want is actually good for your long-term peace of mind.

Once you have thought through your options, the decision is always yours. It is your life. Only you know best how you would like to live it. Only you know what will make you feel peaceful. It is just that sometimes you might not have thought through things in the right manner for a sufficient amount of time, so you might make a decision that pleases you in the short run but does not bring peace in the long run. You may not have run your decisions through your personal, customized decision-making system.

Over the next few pages, you will learn to create such a personal decision-making framework for yourself.

Let us restate our objective:

i. To achieve better clarity of thought,

ii. Using that clarity of thought, make such decisions that lead to a more peaceful mind, and

iii. To be able to find all your answers on your own, independently, without relying on anyone else, forever.

Keep these objectives before you at all times as you undertake this journey. Our goal is to see a conspicuous, measurable positive difference in your state of mind over the next few weeks.

So, as you start practicing these methods, ask yourself every few days:

i. Did I practice for at least ten minutes almost every day?

ii. Have I done this for at least the last three weeks consistently?

iii. Do I see any improvement in my clarity of thought and peace of mind?

iv. Do I see any improvement in my ability to make such decisions that will make me more peaceful?

v. Do I believe I will be able to find all my answers on my own in such a manner that makes me more peaceful, if I were to practice these methods regularly?

We have spoken about two primary problems above. How will we solve those two problems?

The first problem is spending too much time and energy looking outside, and very little looking inward. We will solve this problem by training you in a regular habit of Contemplation.

The second problem is not having a well-defined set of internal guidelines to follow before you decide, personal or professional, mundane or profound. We will solve this problem by providing you with a set of Adios principles and tools that will help you construct your own set of personal guidelines, your own decision-making system, that you will use before making a decision.

Please remember these two steps. Add them to your notes and put a box around them. You will follow this process throughout this book. One, train yourself in regular Contemplation. Two, learn a set of principles on which you can contemplate to make the right decisions in your life.

You will use two other tools during this process – your Vision Planner and the Adioscope. We will explain these as we go along.

What should you expect? When you have practiced the Adios system for some time, you would have become accustomed to regular Contemplation, and you would have a decision-making framework of your own that will help you make your decisions in such a manner that makes you more peaceful. You may not have become a master yet, but that is just a matter of time and more practice. So, what should you expect? You should expect:

i. better clarity of thought,

ii. using that clarity of thought, being able to make such decisions that lead to a more peaceful mind, and

iii. being able to find all your answers independently, on your own, without relying on anyone else, forever.

You should find yourself becoming more thoughtful about what makes you more peaceful and what takes away your peace of mind. You should find yourself choosing thoughts and actions that make you more peaceful. You should find a few of these principles hovering on your mind as you go about your day.

To achieve the above, this is what you need:

- A regular practice of Contemplation, and
- Contemplation on the Adios principles to make your decisions thoughtfully.

Let us now understand what Contemplation is. Then we will explain the Adios principles in detail.

CHAPTER TAKEAWAYS:

- The two key problems today are living your life looking outward and the absence of a personal decision-making system. Contemplation will help you look inward and the Adios principles will help you create your personal decision-making system.

- When you practice this for a few weeks, you will notice a conspicuous improvement in your clarity of thought. You will clearly understand what makes you more peaceful vs less peaceful. You will make your choices in alignment with what brings you long-term peace of mind.

~

3. WHAT IS CONTEMPLATION?

Contemplation is systematic deep thinking – thinking deeply, systematically, about matters that matter.

Contemplation is not the same as thinking. Thinking is the continuous stream of thoughts that go through your mind, consciously or unconsciously. These thoughts may or may not stay for very long in your mind. They may come and go as they please. Contemplation, on the other hand, is:

1. thinking about a particular matter that is important to you
2. very deliberately, intentionally, consciously, by specifically deciding to think about it
3. and also resolving to not think about anything unrelated for the moment
4. thinking about this matter very deeply and systematically
5. using the Adios principles as your guide to think through it
6. thinking deeply with the objective of digging deeper to analyze it, or find an answer, insight, or a solution

7. to find such an answer or solution that makes you peaceful

So, Contemplation is defined as a systematic manner of thinking about something deeply to analyze it in detail using the Adios principles, so you can find such an answer or insight that makes you peaceful.

Contemplation instinctively might seem like a mental activity, but it is both a physical and a mental activity. To start Contemplation, you first need to physically stop doing whatever you were doing if your attention was being consumed by it – speaking to a friend, writing an email, attending an online call, etc. You start with stopping to do what you were doing, then sit on a chair in a quiet room, raise your head by 30 degrees, stare into blankness, and think deeply. You should write your thoughts and analysis as you think deeply using the Adios principles. You should also take a Contemplation walk outside your home or office, thinking about the matter so you can go deeper into it.

If you are thinking about a particular situation in your life, a lot of Contemplation that you will undertake will involve you analyzing that situation using the Adios principles in the Adioscope (discussed later in the book). You should write a lot during this process as writing can sometimes bring about a lot of clarity of thought. But walking Contemplation has its own benefits. It can provide different, and sometimes wider, perspectives to a situation while sitting and writing Contemplation might help you go deeper into a situation. Both are very useful to get to the right answer.

So, you have stepped into your Contemplation session, whether in your room or while on a walk. What do you do next? Depending upon how you feel at that moment, you could try doing the following:

- You can think deeply about a matter that is important to you using the Adios principles. You could solve a real situation from your life using the Adioscope. Adioscope is your personal microscope for life. It is a tool that you will use to analyze your situations, personal or professional. It could be a question about your partner, work, child, home, or any other part of your life. In this case, you start with a specific situation in your life and use the Adioscope to analyze or solve it.
- You can also think about the Adios principles themselves to explore whether they apply to something that is going on in your life currently or something that happened in the past and think about how you could use them to make decisions that will make you more peaceful. In this case, you don't start with a particular situation in your life but instead start with a specific Adios principle and then check if it applies to your past or present life.
- You could spend time with your Vision Planner, re-emphasize the dimensions that are important to you at the moment and resolve to work on them. This will strengthen your inward focus on things that will make you feel more fulfilled and peaceful in the long run.

HOW DOES CONTEMPLATION HELP YOU?

Contemplation on the Adios principles helps you at multiple levels. One, when you start to think deeply about a certain matter, you put in a little extra effort to find your answer. That increases the probability of you finding the answer as against a scenario where you are distracted and not putting in specific time and attention into finding that answer.

Two, when you analyze your situation using the Adios principles, you get a framework to think about that matter systematically. You think about keeping your long term peace of mind rather than short-term satisfaction as your goal. This helps you stay focused and think clearly.

Three, when you run those principles through your mind over and over again during your Contemplation sessions and find the right answers to a few of your questions, your mind starts to get familiarized with your process and gets better at finding the answers that are right for you. This happens because you have thought through these principles multiple times and used them to analyze your situations in life.

As you do this repeatedly, you start to develop a kind of muscle memory and in a few weeks, you consciously feel that you have become much better at the process. Also, these answers are very specific to your life so your mind gets better at finding the answers that work for you. Once you have done it for a few weeks, some of your questions start to resolve even before they are formed. The confusion that might have arisen earlier doesn't arise now because your mind is now clearer at a fundamental level.

As you use these principles repeatedly to think through your real-life situations, they start to get etched on your mind and you will find that after a few weeks, for certain situations, you don't need to spend a lot of time in Contemplation. These principles might be on your mind constantly, operating as an automatic filter to keep your mind clear and peaceful. Certain answers also start to come very effortlessly. This isn't magic. This is the result of your systematic effort and the quality of your Contemplation.

In addition to using Contemplation to find answers to specific questions that you might have – should I enter into / exit this relationship, should I move to a new city, should I take up this job, should I add this product feature, should my kids go to this school, should I go to this party, should I buy this house – you will also find Contemplation exceptionally useful for finding deep insights into whatever you are doing. How is this different from trying to find an answer to a specific question that you might have?

It is different in that in this case, you may not necessarily start with a question already in your mind. You can start with saying – this is what I am working on; can I think deeply about this for a few days and find any new insights about this concept, process, structure, model etc., something that is not visible on the surface, or certain nuances that are buried deep inside.

Concepts (such as gravity and relativity) have been discovered using Contemplation.

Processes in businesses (such as the car assembly line) have been reinvented using Contemplation.

Biological structures (such as those of proteins and DNA) have been understood using Contemplation.

Business models (such as those for music and urban transportation) have been reimagined using Contemplation.

Communication tools (such as the internet and computers) have been developed using Contemplation.

A pharma or biotech company could train their R&D team in Contemplation to discover a new molecule. Currently, most companies do not really have a specific process to create innovation. They largely rely on repeated experimentation and group discussion. Adding systematic Contemplation training will increase the probability and frequency of making newer and better discoveries. Contemplation can help you create innovation at will, wherever and whenever you want, in a systematic and repeatable manner, quarter on quarter.

Multilateral institutions such as the UN, WHO, World Bank, IMF, etc. can train their teams in Contemplation to find creative answers to large global problems such as hunger, health, poverty, climate change and financial crisis management and prevention. Such deep problems need deep thinking - the ability to stare into blankness for long periods of time.

Business schools can train their students in Contemplation to solve case studies in a more thoughtful manner. Contemplation Labs can become part of the curriculum. This will take case analysis discussions to a whole new level.

Investors and financial institutions can train their founders, leaders and employees in the Adios principles to insure themselves against future financial fraud. Every financial fraud starts in the mind. Some of your founders or employees might be planning to commit one right now as you read this. You can nip a fraud in the bud if you have trained those minds in the Adios principles.

An Artificial Intelligence (AI) company can train their engineers in Contemplation on the Adios principles to enable them to think in a manner that leads to fulfilling, purposeful and peaceful outcomes. This will ensure that AI is used for the right purposes. Regulations will always lag behind the sharp human mind. If you are really serious about achieving the benevolent AI goal, you need to tackle the problem at the level of that sharp human mind itself. You need engineers with inner clarity and a mind that has learned to focus on living a fulfilling, meaningful and peaceful life rather than a mind that is focused on short-term pleasure and excitement. What your mind believes, your body delivers. What their mind believes, their fingers will deliver.

Schools can train their kids in Contemplation to help them become deeper thinkers, especially in an era where they might be tempted to use AI to do their homework. AI can help them improve and magnify their intelligence, but only Contemplation can help them use their own uniqueness and deep thought to create something that doesn't exist today. Contemplation is a critical life skill that will also enable them to make the right decisions in life, and in some cases, save them from making terrible decisions that might be dangerous for their physical or emotional health.

Profound truths about life in general, and your own life in particular, can be found using Contemplation. Answers to less profound, day-to-day questions can be found using Contemplation on the Adios principles. You can find these answers yourself, on your own, without relying on anyone else. Forever. If you train your inner counselor, you will never need to depend on an external one. Contemplation is your tool to do that.

Contemplation is the mother of clarity.

4. YOUR TOOLS - VISION PLANNER AND ADIOSCOPE

Recall the process you will follow. One, training yourself in regular Contemplation. Two, learning a set of Adios principles on which you can contemplate so you can make the right decisions.

The Adios principles are your practical tools that you will use to find your answers. You will apply these principles to analyze your real-life situations and find the answer that is right for you.

The objective of doing this is to be able to find an answer that makes you more peaceful in the long run. You will make these decisions yourself, without relying on anyone else. It is your life. You need to decide what makes you more peaceful, what makes you less peaceful or more restless, and accordingly decide what you want to do in a particular situation in your life and why.

These principles will help you construct your own internal set of guidelines, your moral compass, your personal decision-making system that you can use as you navigate relationships, work, parenting, health, finances and other important aspects, transitions and challenges in your life.

The goal is to become independent in terms of finding all your answers yourself, without relying on anyone else, forever.

You will also use two other devices in this process - your Vision Planner and the Adioscope.

Before you implement your Vision Planner, you need to incorporate the concept of the Adios year into your life. Your Adios year runs from your birthday to birthday. You can plan your life according to your Adios year, rather than the calendar year. Instead of making new year resolutions along with the whole wide world, you can plan your life based on your Adios year, birthday to birthday. Your Adios year is much more relevant and personal to you.

For example, if your birthday is on September 5, then your Adios year will run from Sep 5 to Sep 4 each year. You can then break this down into quarters and months to plan your life in more detail using the Vision Planner. So your quarters will end on December 4, March 4 and June 4.

Vision Planner

You will start your Adios journey by defining your Vision Planner. Your Vision Planner will have three tiers:

- Dimension

- Goal

- Task

Dimension

The Dimension defines areas in your life that you would like to work on at the moment. While there might be many dimensions in one's life – intellectual growth, relationship, work, hobby, parenting, health, finances, self, etc., you will define the dimensions that are currently important to you.

Dimensions that are important usually change as we go along. For someone young, the dimensions that might be more relevant to them at that stage of life might be education and relationships, and not so much work and parenting. For someone at a different stage in life, this might change.

If you recently stepped out of a relationship, regaining your emotional health or clarity might be more important at the moment. If you have been working for a while but find yourself dissatisfied, finding work that is more meaningful for you might be more important at this stage. Similarly, if you have been looking to be in a stable, peaceful relationship but have been mostly finding people who are only interested in short-term associations, gaining clarity on that dimension might be your priority.

Please start by defining two or three dimensions that are currently important to you. You can do this right now. Write this down in your Vision Planner. Trying to work on too many dimensions at the same time generally means you don't do justice to any of them. Pick a couple or so, and then use Contemplation and the Adios principles as your tools to go deep inside your mind in order to find clarity and make some real progress on those dimensions. Once you do that with a certain dimension, you can then revise your Vision Planner and work on certain other dimensions important to you.

Goal

Under each dimension, you will define a particular goal for yourself. For instance, under the dimension "Intellectual Growth", you might state one of your goals as "Improve my knowledge in <this particular topic>". Under the dimension "Physical Fitness", you might have a goal that says, "Lose weight" or "Sleep better".

You could define multiple goals under each dimension. Again, let your current phase of life help you decide that. Think deeply about what will make you feel more fulfilled, purposeful and peaceful in the next 3-6 months and put that on your Vision Planner. You can also add something longer term to the list.

Task

Under each Goal, you will define quantifiable tasks to achieve that goal. The tasks need to be quantifiable – very specific and objective. "Walk for 45 minutes in the evening", "Complete the XYZ program online", or "Learn to play Songs A and B on the piano" are tasks that are specific – quantifiable. "Play the piano regularly" is less specific.

The task needs to be specific and measurable. So, under the dimension "Mental Fitness", one of your goals could be "Achieve better clarity of thought and peace of mind" and "Get better at finding all my answers myself", and the tasks to achieve those goals could be "Go for a Contemplation walk for 30 minutes a day", "Spend time with my Vision Planner every Sunday for 30 minutes", and "Analyze two Adioscope situations each week".

You complete the tasks each week, which should lead to the completion of the goal, which should lead to progress on that particular dimension. But throughout this journey, remember your north star - peace of mind.

Vision Planner Example:

Dimension: Career Growth

Goal 1: Increase my professional skills in my field of work.

Tasks:

1) Attend one professional development conference related to my field.

2) Enroll in an online course to learn a new skill relevant to my job.

3) Participate in a mentorship program to gain insights and guidance from experienced professionals.

Goal 2: Build a strong professional network in my industry.

Tasks:

1) Attend at least two industry networking events and conferences.

2) Connect with ten new people on LinkedIn every week and schedule informational interviews.

3) Join a professional association in my field and attend their events.

Dimension: Health & Wellness

Goal 1: Improve my physical health.

Tasks:

1) Exercise for at least 30 minutes each day.

2) Eat a balanced and nutritious diet, incorporating more fruits and vegetables. Reduce junk food to twice a week.

3) Get 7-8 hours of uninterrupted sleep each night.

Goal 2: Enhance my mental well-being and reduce stress.

Tasks:

1) Read one chapter from this book daily.

2) Analyze at least two Adioscope situations every week.

3) Go for a 30 min Contemplation walk every morning or evening.

Example Vision Planner for a Parent:

Dimension: Parenting

Goal 1: Improve my bond with my daughter.

Task 1: Have a conversation with her every day for at least 30 minutes about her day and feelings and be fully present during that conversation without being distracted by technology.

Task 2: Attend a parenting workshop to learn new communication strategies

Task 3: Go to a park once a week along with her.

Goal 2: Create a positive home environment.

Task 1: 20 mins of Contemplation practice each day. Apply the Adios principles to ensure I stay calm and composed myself and set the right example for my child.

Task 2: Organize a weekly family game night to have some fun time together.

Task 3: Ensure my language stays polite at home and outside. No profanity, even when I am angry.

Task 4: Stop watching TV series that contain foul language.

You can always revise and adjust your Vision Planner based on changes in your life and priorities. The goal is to get started and then make changes if necessary as you go along. Don't forget to organize your Vision Planner in accordance with your Adios year. Plan it until your next birthday by breaking it up into months and quarters, and then plan the next full year. Your Adios year keeps the process relevant, unique and relatable.

Adioscope

The Adioscope is like your personal microscope for life. During your Contemplation sessions, you will use the Adioscope to analyze a real-life situation in your life by running it through your Adioscope. The Adioscope provides you with a step-by-step decision-making framework.

As you go through the chapters in this book, you will come across multiple Adioscope situations of people from various walks of life and you will learn how they analyzed those situations systematically using the Adioscope to resolve them and find an answer that is right for them at that point in their life. Their specific answer is irrelevant. Focus on the process.

The Adioscope is designed to help you take a particular real-life situation or question through the various Adios principles to help you think through that situation with respect to each Adios principle and achieve better clarity of thought as a result. Certain principles may apply to your situation and others may not. That is almost always the case.

Sometimes, just one or two principles apply to your situation so strongly that you find the clarity you were looking for and you need not look any further. In certain other instances, you may Adioscope a situation multiple times using multiple principles and peel the layers of the onion gradually to get to the final state of clarity. You will enjoy the process and learn a lot in either case.

The goal of Adios is to help you be independent in terms of finding your own answers, forever. The Adioscope is your companion to help you do that. Through Contemplation on the Adios principles, you will appreciate deeply what makes you feel more fulfilled, purposeful and peaceful, which will help you make decisions that will help you feel that way. On your own. Without relying on anyone else. This is true independence.

Train your inner counselor using Contemplation and you may never need to excessively depend on an external one. Ever. The key to this is going slow. Your instinct might tell you to go fast and absorb everything quickly but doing it quickly doesn't allow it to go deeper. So let the principles sink in slowly. Don't rush. It isn't about you going through the principles. It is about the principles going through you. Go for your Contemplation walks regularly. Think about them over and over and you will start to feel the change.

So here is our plan. As you go through the book, please contemplate on:

a. The situations in your Adioscope

b. The Adios Principles

c. Your Vision Planner

Do this for three weeks slowly and regularly, and you will start to see something inside of you change for the better. I assure you.

Now let us learn a few Adios principles. As you go through the principles, please think of certain situations from your past or present and apply these principles to those situations. Your goal is to use these principles to be able to think more clearly and make such decisions that leave you more peaceful.

CHAPTER TAKEAWAYS:

- The Adios principles, the Vision Planner, and the Adioscope are your tools to find clarity of thought and peace of mind. A regular Contemplation on these will keep your mind clear and peaceful.
- Plan your life using your Adios year rather than the standard Jan to Dec calendar year. Your Adios year runs from your birthday to birthday. It is more relevant and relatable to you.

∾

PART TWO: THE ADIOS PRINCIPLES

5. PRINCIPLE ONE: THE TWIN VOICES

It sounds very poetic to say, 'you must listen to your inner voice', but that isn't enough. You need to dig deeper and ask - which inner voice?

You have multiple voices inside of you, and all of those are your inner voices. Some of those voices may be louder than others, but many a time, the loudest voice is not necessarily the right voice.

If you are focused too much on money, your inner voice might encourage you to lie to others to make more money or to take up a job only because it pays well. If you are hungry for fame, your inner voice might make you do or say things so that you gain the attention of others. If you are insecure about your abilities or jealous about someone else's, your inner voice might encourage you to be rude to others or even beat them so you can feel good about yourself temporarily. But at the same time, you might have another voice that might be saying - This is not right. Don't do it.

So you need to be clear - which of these inner voices must you listen to? Which voice is actually right for you? How do you decide what is right for you?

By observing your mind and actions on a regular basis, you will understand them much better. Very often in a situation, you might notice that you have two voices inside your head. One might say do this while the other might say do that. In some cases, there could be more than two voices. You must learn to differentiate between the voices that make you feel less peaceful or more restless and those that make you more peaceful.

Through your Contemplation practice you will develop the ability to clearly understand which voices improve your well-being and which reduce your peace of mind. By consciously choosing the voice that aligns with your long-term inner peace, you take ownership of your mind and make the right decision every time.

By understanding the multiple voices within, you will gain the ability as well as the confidence necessary to make your life's choices with complete clarity. That is what matters. Clarity is everything. If you know exactly what you must do in each situation, why you must do it, and are confident which decision will make you feel more fulfilled, purposeful and peaceful, there is no power bigger than that. That's true independence.

By using the Adioscope as your Contemplation tool, you can examine your mind deeply, break down the situation you are analyzing into manageable components, use the Adios principles to think through each component and finally make the right decision - a decision that is right for you at that point in time, in that phase of your life, even though it may not be right for a friend or colleague. A decision that will make you feel more peaceful.

What should I do? This is a question you will face regularly in your life.

At various times during the day, you might need to make certain decisions. These decisions could be about yourself, your partner, your kids, your work, your team members, your superior, your voting preference, your health, finances or any other dimension in your life. The decision could be about:

- which city you would like to live in
- the kind of home you should have
- the interiors inside your home
- the music you want to listen to
- the movies/TV series you must watch
- the physical exercise you would like to do
- the clothes you would like to wear
- the food you would like to eat
- what you should drink
- the kind of friends you would like to have
- the kind of partner you should have in your life
- what to say or do and what not to in your relationship with your partner
- whether or when to have kids and how to raise them
- whom to vote for or what causes to support on an ongoing basis

Many, many decisions. Each day. All your life.

For many of these decisions, you might be faced with multiple alternatives to choose from. You might hear two voices in your head. One voice might say - do this and the other might say - no, do that instead. Sometimes you could hear multiple voices in that situation. These voices could present mildly different perspectives or alternatives, and sometimes strongly opposing or contradictory paths.

You are your strongest mental voice. That is who you really are. So, you must understand these voices and know which one dominates you. If you do not pay attention to them, you might never get to know yourself truly. You might just go with the flow and let your dominant voice rule your entire life, even if it isn't healthy for your long-term peace of mind and that of your loved ones. Many people go through their entire life in that manner without realizing it. It is quite common today so don't think 'But I would never do that'. If you don't pay careful attention to your mental voices and live your life mostly plugged into the outside world, it is quite likely that you will fall into that trap too.

Some voices can uplift you while some others can completely drain your energy. Some can leave you more joyful while some others can leave you without a smile on your face. These voices reflect your desires, fears, doubts, emotions, insecurities, reasoning, and other aspects of your personality, and play a significant role in deciding what you choose to do.

You need to get familiar with each of these voices. These are your voices. This is your mind presenting alternatives or perspectives to you. Just because it is your mind does not mean that it always thinks in such a manner as to improve your peace of mind. You might notice that in some cases, it is quite the opposite. It might sometimes present choices to you that are not right for you in the short term, or sometimes not right for you in the long-term, and sometimes absolutely disastrous for you in the short and the long-term.

You must understand that your mind does not always operate with the intention of enhancing your long-term well-being. In fact, your mind can often deceive you and lead you down the wrong road if you are not vigilant. Your mind is not your friend every time. It can be, but for that you need to know your mind really well. You need to be in charge. You need to constantly choose the right mental voice that should drive your decisions. If you aren't paying attention, your loudest mental voice might take over your life, which is not always the right voice.

Think about what is happening in your life currently. What happened over the last few days at home, at work, or outside home? Do you remember giving in to the wrong voice and doing or saying something that made you less peaceful?

Think.

Deeply.

Your primary purpose in this journey of Adios is to get to know your mind well. Your goal is to understand exactly what you are thinking and doing and how it affects your long-term peace of mind. You need to know which voice is largely driving your life today, and if that is the right voice for you.

Your mind is a clever trickster. If you are not smart enough, it can play havoc in your life. So be aware. Be in charge. You need to own your mind, and not the other way around. That is why you need to understand it very well. How else will you be in charge?

Ownership of your mind can only be achieved through a deep understanding of its inner workings. In a particular situation, your mind is essentially the multiple voices in your head. You must understand the two, or more than two, voices you might hear in that situation. You should be able to identify and write them out clearly. In a certain situation, say, if your question is - Should I move from LA to San Francisco - you should be able to clearly understand what each voice is saying and write them down as:

Voice 1 says do this (stay in LA, I have great friends here, a good job, why uproot myself and disturb my life?)

Voice 2 says do that (move to San Francisco, a new city, newer possibilities for work, a fresh environment will get me out of my boring routine)

Voice 3 says do this instead (give up my current busy city life and move to a small, quiet town in Spain away from the noise, write a book, explore nature, spend time with family)

These voices often reflect different motivations and perspectives. They may also represent different groups of people. One voice may be driven by fear, constantly warning you of potential dangers and pitfalls. This could also be the voice of the society consisting of all the standard expectations your society has from you - get a stable job, make a lot of money, have a big house, demonstrate worldly success.

Another voice might be the voice of a bully at school or an unhealthy boss at work, rooted in self-doubt, undermining your confidence, and preventing you from pursuing your dreams. There may also be a voice of reason, providing logical analysis and objective viewpoints. Another voice could be influenced by what's happening in the world today and wanting you to imitate others. One voice could be telling you to do what will excite you at the moment. Another voice could be telling you what will make you feel more fulfilled and peaceful in the long run.

By recognizing these different voices, you understand multiple motivations that might determine your thoughts and actions. You get to know the fears and insecurities that hold you back. But you also know what will ultimately make you feel more fulfilled, purposeful and peaceful in the long run - the most important voice inside of you. Only you can know what makes you feel that way. But you will never know if you never ask.

When was the last time you asked yourself - What makes me feel more peaceful? Not happy. Not excited. Peaceful. Do it as often as possible.

As you deepen your understanding of the voices within, you will begin to clearly identify which ones contribute to your well-being and which ones obstruct your progress as a human being. This clarity allows you to consciously choose the voice that brings you closer to inner peace.

Remember, you are your dominant voice, so you must be aware of all the voices and choose your dominant voice carefully. That will define the quality of your relationship, your work, your parenting, your health, and everything else. The dominant voice may also be different in different situations, with different people, in different environments. So be aware.

How will you choose which voice to follow? Choose the one that makes you feel more peaceful in the long run. If you examine your Twin Voices with respect to certain situations in your daily life regularly, you will soon get better at identifying them in real time, as the situation is taking place. You will also get better at explaining them clearly. Once you can write them down clearly, it becomes easier to choose the one that is right for you.

Understanding your inner dialogue requires some patience and practice. It is common to experience conflicting voices and the temptation to fall back into old patterns of thought, do something you are used to doing, or something that is easier to do. But with consistent Contemplation practice, you will gradually start to choose the voice that makes you more peaceful. That is the goal.

You might experience some fogginess in your thinking initially, but with regular Contemplation practice, you will sharpen your ability to identify the voices as soon as they arise. You will become an expert at clearly articulating them and recognizing their impact on your daily actions at home, work and other situations. This clarity will empower you to choose the voice that guides you toward inner peace.

It is possible that when you start your Contemplation practice and analyze situations in your life using your Adioscope, you might initially reduce your peace of mind for some time instead of increasing it. This could be because all of a sudden you might have tens of things coming up inside your mind at the same time from the past or the present. You might have avoided facing certain issues in the past or chosen to forget them, but now that you are analyzing your past, these may come up and disturb your mind. Don't worry about this.

This is similar to a situation where water in a glass might appear to be clear not because it is really clear but because all the dirt is settled at the bottom of the glass. When you start to stir it, all that dirt comes up. Similarly, if you had things buried at the bottom of your mind because you chose to ignore them, they might come up during your Contemplation practice. Don't avoid them again. This time, consider each disturbing element that comes up, study it and resolve it once and for all using Contemplation on the Adios principles. Clean up all the dirt this time for good, so there is nothing left to settle at the bottom of your glass.

Once you get clarity on these situations, you will be left with a lighter, clearer and more peaceful mind that is ready to take on newer challenging situations in the future, but this time with tremendous confidence saying:

'I now know how to find the right answers in my life so I am not worried. I may not know the answer today, but I know how to find it, and this time the answer will be one that makes me more fulfilled and peaceful.'

You might also choose to classify these voices in your head. For example, you could call the two voices the voice of the head and the voice of the heart. Sometimes, you might tend to lean toward the voice of the head too much and ignore the voice of the heart. While that might be the right thing to do in certain cases, many a time you might do that because someone else wants you to do so (peer, family or societal pressure), or because you are afraid you might fail (emotion), or because that is what most other people around you usually do (imitation), or because you feel others might judge you harshly (fear of judgment), or some other such reason.

Learn to understand and express your inner voices clearly and choose the one that makes you more peaceful in the long run.

Pause for a minute and ask yourself - In which dimensions of my life today can I apply the principle of the Twin Voices? In my relationship? At work? With my children?

If you are a business leader, are you facing a situation right now where you have multiple voices about a critical decision you need to make? Following which voice will make you feel more peaceful in the long run? Which voice might give you short-term satisfaction or relief today but may not be right for the long run?

Do you have a situation about your relationship with your partner where you can hear multiple voices inside of you? Or about your kids? What are they saying?

Think of a situation in your past where the voice of your head won over the voice of your heart even though you believed then or you believe today that you should have followed your heart because you feel it was the right thing to do.

Why was that the right thing to do for you?

Would doing that make you more peaceful?

Why were you not able to do it?

Would you like to do it now, better late than never?

As you read through the following Adioscopes, think of a situation in your life today where you need to make a decision by choosing from different options. Use this principle to analyze the multiple voices inside your head about that situation. Contemplation is about doing, not knowing, or understanding. The more Adioscope situations you solve, the better your Contemplation muscle will become.

So, open up a new document and write a few situations in your life that you wish to analyze, past or current. You might find some answers before you finish reading this book.

In which dimensions of your life today can you apply the ADIOS principle of The Twin Voices?

ROSA'S ADIOSCOPE

Situation

I'm looking for a partner for myself. I like someone but he's from a different cultural and religious background than me. We really hit it off, but I'm unsure about pursuing a relationship because of our different backgrounds. My family has always emphasized sticking to our own community. My friends seem skeptical too. He's open to making it work, but going against my upbringing makes me doubt myself.

Twin Voices:

1. Do I have multiple voices inside of me about this situation? Are they presenting me with multiple options to be pursued in this situation? If yes, what are those options?

Yes, I do hear multiple voices in my head about this dilemma. Voice 1 says: "Commit to Benny because he is charming, fun to be around, and can bring excitement to your life." Voice 2 says: "Take your time to get to know Benny better before committing to him. Evaluate if you two are truly compatible and if the relationship has the potential for long-term happiness and peace of mind." Voice 3 is saying "What will my family say about this? They may never accept him."

1. Which of those options would make me more peaceful in the long run, if I were to follow that Voice and do as it says?

Following Voice 2 would make me more peaceful in the long run. By taking the time to get to know Benny better and evaluating our compatibility, I would be making a more informed decision about whether to commit to him, which will ultimately lead to greater peace and happiness in the long term. If I find him to be the right guy for me, I think I can convince my family to come around eventually. They want me to be happy after all.

But I don't want my decision to be based on short-term excitement. Sure, we have fun together and that feels good. But I have similar fun with many other friends of mine. I am not going to marry any of them. I want my decision to be based on whether Benny and I share a similar value system at a fundamental level and whether we are largely aligned in terms of what a fulfilling and peaceful life together means. If we define such a life very differently, then I need to be careful about committing to him.

Twin Voices about Work

Let us say you work at an organization, and you have received an offer from another organization to join them. Depending upon your unique situation, here are a few possible voices you might hear in your head. Which ones do you hear in your head?

1. I am comfortable here in this organization. I have created good relationships with my peers, superiors, and subordinates. The compensation is fair. The work is not too bad. Why move?

2. I need more experience because I want to grow in my career. I may not get that here.

3. I am not happy here. While the compensation is good, the culture is not very healthy. The founders have lost touch with

themselves and their initial vision that inspired me. Now they only care about money.

4. We are just about to start doing great things here after working hard for the last few months. The culture is fantastic. We are working toward something I believe in. Should I leave at such a time?

5. I have always wanted to move to that organization for a long time. It is a dream for anyone to work there. I may never get another chance.

6. My boss is really making me feel small all the time. I have spent the last few months doubting my own capabilities. I think I am quite good at my work and my colleagues get along well with me. But the negativity of my boss is declining my self-esteem. This job seems like a good opportunity to get away from this toxic environment.

7. I have just been handed an interesting profile with independent responsibility. I personally like the project and it will teach me a lot. Probably not the right time to leave.

8. That organization might be offering me better compensation, but I have heard they do not have a very healthy value system. Anything goes so long as you can get money in the door. The culture here is great. Do I really want to prioritize financial growth over mental peace?

9. I really need to get out of this city and this seems like a good opportunity to do that. The offered compensation might not be significantly higher but it allows me to move cities.

10. My kids go to a great school here and that will get disrupted if I move to that organization. Do I really want to take that chance?

11. My parents are ill and need assistance. I really need the money at this point. I should move.

12. My friends have been growing in their profession much faster than I have, but I know I have more depth and knowledge than they do because I don't hop jobs at the drop of a hat for better compensation. That improves my self-worth. It's too early to leave.

As you can see, depending upon your phase of life and your specific work situation, your mental voices can vary significantly. These were just a few possibilities. You might have other voices about your work. Only you can find the voice that is right for you, the one that will make you feel more fulfilled, purposeful, and peaceful.

Ask yourself:

- Does my work add meaning to my life or is it just a means to pay the bills?
- Do I have a personal non-financial vision for my work life and does my current work help me achieve that vision?
- Am I too focused on keeping others happy rather than doing what I feel is right?
- If I think about my work right now for a second, does every cell of my body say - Yes this is what you should be doing. This will bring you long-term fulfillment and peace of mind.
- Am I sure I am not working on something that might feel exciting and important at the moment but will eventually reduce people's well-being and peace of mind?

If you have a question or concern about your work or organization, Contemplation on the Adios principles using the Adioscope is the way to find that right answer.

RACHEL'S ADIOSCOPE

Situation

I've become disengaged at work, just going through the motions without passion. I used to love my job, but now I've lost my drive. I'm only here for the monthly paycheck. I don't like this feeling at all.

Twin Voices:

Voice 1: Start exploring new hobbies and activities outside of work. Try joining a local club, taking up a new sport, or learning a new skill. This will help me find new interests and passions that might reignite my drive.

Voice 2: Consider looking for a new job or a new role within my current company. A change in my work environment and responsibilities might provide the challenge I need to regain my enthusiasm.

Which of those options would make me more peaceful in the long run, if I were to follow that Voice and do as it says?

Following Voice 1 and exploring new hobbies and activities outside of work could lead to a more balanced and fulfilling life. By pursuing my interest in singing, I may find a renewed sense of purpose that could break the monotony and help me get energized about my work.

On the other hand, following Voice 2 and seeking a new job or role within my current company might directly address the issue of feeling stuck in my career. This change could provide the challenge and growth opportunities I need to feel satisfied in my professional life.

I think the best option for my long-term peace may be a combination of both voices: working on my singing while also looking for another job. This time, I want to be careful about the kind of company and culture I choose. I want to thrive at my work, so I end each day with a smile, and I don't have to slip out of the office like a thief at the end of the day. That feels terrible.

In every area of your life, you need to understand the voices inside your head well so you can make the right decision for yourself, the decision that will make you more peaceful in the long run. Only you can know what will make you feel that way. You can take suggestions or guidance from others, but use Contemplation to make your decision yourself.

The final decisions of the protagonists in these Adioscopes is irrelevant. Not only can the answers be different for different people, but the same question also asked by the same person might yield three completely different right answers depending upon their specific situation and phase of life, depending upon what is right for them, what makes them peaceful, at that point in time.

So as you read these Adioscopes, start constructing your own Adioscopes about a few situations in your life and try resolving them using the principles in this book.

Chapter Takeaways:

- Learn to identify and differentiate between multiple voices inside your head. Choose the voice that makes you more peaceful in the long run.
- Use your Adioscope to analyze your real-life situations using the Adios principles. Write a lot in your Adioscope.
- Sometimes, the process of Contemplation can initially lead to a temporary decrease in peace of mind as past, unresolved or buried issues resurface. Don't worry about it. Use the Adios principles to resolve them once and for all to achieve a lighter, more peaceful mind. This mind

can then confidently handle complex situations in the future.

- Do you have an important decision to make at the moment? Do you hear multiple voices inside your head about that decision? What are they saying? Which one will make you more peaceful in the long run?

6. PRINCIPLE TWO: THE URGE TO PROVE

In your personal interactions at home, or at work or social gatherings, or on an online forum, you might experience an urge to prove that you are right or someone else is wrong. It usually comes from a desire to be recognized or respected by others or to gain their attention or validation, or sometimes to overpower a deep-rooted feeling of inferiority that sits within.

When you prove someone else wrong, you experience a kind of psychological victory in that moment that makes you feel good about yourself. But it usually leaves you more restless. It takes away your peace of mind.

This can happen when you become too emotionally attached to your own ideas and opinions. It then becomes a mission to get others to see your perspective, and more importantly, to accept that your perspective is the right one. This can also make it difficult for you to pay attention to the perspectives of others because your focus now is not on learning or expanding your knowledge but on establishing that you are right. If someone else's ideas contradict yours, those become even harder to consider, and sometimes deliver a blow to your ego.

As we have said earlier, your overarching goal is to become more peaceful, which means the absence of stress, anxiety, and restlessness. If you give in to your urge to prove frequently, it tends to leave you more restless, so less peaceful. You need to pay attention to it, ask yourself how you feel when you give in to this urge - do I feel more peaceful or more restless - and accordingly decide what you must do.

When you frequently give in to the urge to prove, at home during a conversation with your partner, or your child, or your parent, or with a colleague at work, or someone at a social function, or during an online conversation, you unconsciously invite restlessness into your life, pushing you further away from the inner peace that you seek. It is crucial for you to pay attention to this urge and ask how it truly makes you feel—does it make you more peaceful or less peaceful?

The urge to prove is deeply ingrained in the human mind. It is a very natural human tendency so don't waste your time feeling guilty about it. If it does occur, pay attention to what it does to your peace of mind and if it makes you less peaceful, decide to work on eliminating it from your speech.

At the core of this urge lies your desire for recognition, respect, and attention. When you yearn to be seen and acknowledged for your intellect, capabilities, and accomplishments, it might give rise to an impatience to prove it to others. This craving for validation is driven by a fundamental need of your mind to feel significant and valued by others. However, it's important to recognize that seeking external validation through proving can become a never-ending cycle that ultimately leaves you restless and unsatisfied.

Also note here that your mind is not always your best friend. It might naturally look for external appreciation or validation, but that doesn't mean it is good for you. Your mind has multiple voices and one of those voices could be your urge to prove others wrong. But there also might be another voice that makes you more peaceful. Find that voice.

Deep-rooted feelings of inferiority also often contribute to your urge to prove yourself. These feelings very often arise from comparing yourself negatively with others (see the chapter on Negative Comparison). The need to prove your superiority or correctness can arise as a defense mechanism to compensate for these feelings of inadequacy.

When you successfully prove someone else wrong, you may experience a fleeting sense of psychological victory. Your mind might feel good in the moment. You might feel a surge of confidence and satisfaction, as if you have triumphed over the other person. However, this victory is often short-lived and almost always fails to bring lasting peace of mind. It usually takes it away. You might feel for a moment that you have won a battle, but rest assured, you are losing the war. Every time you give in to that urge, picture yourself adding drops of black paint in a bucket of white paint. You are adding restlessness to your life. Keep adding those black drops, and slowly the white will turn into light gray, then dark gray and eventually...Time's up.

A constant urge to prove yourself reinforces your lower self-worth in your mind subconsciously, so you continue to seek new opportunities to prove yourself, and the vicious cycle goes on. If you aren't asking yourself - Is this impatience making me more peaceful or less peaceful, years might pass without you noticing what that urge is doing to your own peace of mind. You may start to love the short-term high and the surge of instant satisfaction it gives you. You may start to mistake domination for victory. But it arises from an illusion of superiority. The reality is that you have become an external appreciation addict.

In your personal relationships, the desire to be right all the time can lead to persistent stress and restlessness. Whether it's a disagreement with a partner, family member, or friend, the urge to prove your point not only keeps you less peaceful but often escalates tensions and damages the foundation of your relationship.

During a discussion about future plans, instead of listening and considering your partner's perspective respectfully, you might insist on your own ideas, dismissing their thoughts. This insistence on being right might not only leave you less peaceful but can also create emotional distance between you and your partner and eventually lead to an unhappy relationship which might further reduce your peace of mind. Yes, your mind might get you to behave in this manner, but you now know that your mind does not always work in favor of your long-term inner peace. The loudest voice in your mind is not necessarily the right one. You need to take charge and decide what that loudest voice should be.

At the workplace, the urge to prove your superiority can arise from a desire for recognition, respect or promotion. When you focus on proving your competence by working together as a team in a healthy, collaborative manner, you create more restlessness on your inside and an uncomfortable environment on the outside. This not only diminishes your own peace of mind but also creates an unhealthy work environment.

For example, in a conversation, do you constantly interrupt and dismiss others' ideas to prove your own superiority or speak to them in a tone that is disrespectful, patronizing or sarcastic? Does that make you feel more peaceful, or does it take away your peace of mind?

The urge to prove your parenting methods as superior can create unnecessary stress and tension inside of you as well as between you and your child or your partner. When you focus on being dominating in parenting decisions, you may lose sight of your child's individual needs and preferences, and sometimes the perspectives of your partner in that matter. Are you trying to assert your authority because you have a hidden need to feel powerful over them? Are you trying to realize an unfulfilled dream of yours through your child but justifying it by saying 'I am only looking out for you' without really considering what might be good for their own well-being?

If you are pregnant, you should be extremely careful about your mental environment during and after your pregnancy because it directly affects the long-term development of your child. You need to ensure that you can think clearly and make choices that help you remain calm and peaceful. You should make this book part of your pregnancy care routine.

A restless mind can do enormous harm to your inner peace and external relationships. Through a regular habit of Contemplation, take your time to think deeply about what will make your personal and professional life more fulfilling, purposeful, and peaceful and choose your actions accordingly.

In music, the urge to prove your musical preferences as superior, for example classical music vs other genres, can create unnecessary restlessness inside of you. It can also lead to social conflicts and keep you from enjoying diverse genres which could have led to expanding your musical experiences that might have helped you maximize your potential or add to your fulfillment.

If you are a leader but are disconnected from yourself because you have lived your life largely focused on the external world, you might be tempted to prove others wrong or overpower a conversation to experience a sense of control over others. Silencing the room by raising your voice might feel very empowering. If only you could read the minds of the silenced. Respect is always earned, never demanded. Spending time alone with yourself and with these principles, quietly, without discussing with anyone else, will help you create a deeper connection with yourself, and enable you to lead with a calm conviction that will inspire a room, not intimidate it.

For a moment of excitement, don't sacrifice your long-term peace of mind. Pay attention to such an urge if it surfaces during the day at home or outside and control it so you can act in a manner that provides you with a greater sense of inner peace.

In which dimensions of your life today can you apply the ADIOS principle of The Urge to Prove?

_____

_____

_____

MAYA'S ADIOSCOPE:

Situation

I was too critical of others in a team meeting. I thought I was being smart, but I was just being mean. This made people uncomfortable and not want to share ideas. This attitude is hurting my relationship with my colleagues.

Twin Voices:

I can hear two voices within me—the critical voice and the empathetic voice.

That critical voice in my head was in full force when I shot down John's idea at the meeting. I focused on poking holes in his suggestion instead of considering any potential value it could add. That voice was all about showing off how smart I am by dominating others. My tone was really condescending and harsh - no wonder John looked insulted and discouraged.

But I know I've also got an empathetic side that cares about recognizing people's efforts and understanding different views. That part of me wants to build a warm, collaborative vibe on the team.

I want to follow Voice 2, the empathetic voice, but my critical voice is so deeply engraved in my personality that I will need to work at it seriously and eliminate it. And I do see it now that the critical voice actually makes me less peaceful, even though it might give me a temporary boost of ego when I use it. I think it is deteriorating the overall quality of my life.

Edit (10 mins later): Now that I think about it, I also tend to carry this attitude home and sometimes the bedroom turns into a battle room.

The Urge to Prove:

I gotta be real - throughout that whole meeting, I had this major urge to show off how smart I am. I just wanted to prove I'm the most brilliant one in the room. While I was faking being professional on the outside, this is what was really going on in my mind. And that totally caused me to act rude and condescending to my colleagues.

I'm seeing now how this need to be right and superior puts up huge blinders for me. It makes me hyper-focused on myself versus thinking about others at all. And it's definitely poisoning my personal and professional relationships.

Chasing that ego boost does not actually leave me feeling peaceful - it just amps me up and stresses me out. I want to change this pattern going forward. I'm gonna consciously drop that overly self-centered mentality. Instead, I'll focus on being friendly, warm and collaborative with my teammates.

This will not only help me feel more peaceful day-to-day, but also make our work more positive and enjoyable. Boosting my ego may give a temporary rush, but it's not worth sacrificing real connections and happiness. Being part of a team matters more than always needing to be the star player.

Edit (10 minutes later): And hopefully after this change, the bedroom will continue to remain a bedroom.

EMILY'S ADIOSCOPE

Situation

I've gotten completely obsessed with being successful at my marketing job. I'm relentlessly chasing achievements and promotions, never feeling like I've done enough. My coworkers notice that I never take breaks or go out with them. I just stay late at the office every night, my personal life sacrificed for work.

My boss warned me that I'm pushing myself too hard and need more balance to avoid burnout. But I insisted I can handle it - I just want to be the best at what I do, no matter the cost. She told me that being excellent doesn't mean working nonstop.

I know my boss is right. My obsession with success has taken over my life. I need to learn how to maintain boundaries and take care of myself, not just focus on being the best employee. Excellence requires balance, not burnout. I want to improve, but old habits die hard.

The urge to prove can also slip into your conversations with your kids, friends and other loved ones. It can raise its head at a party or a conference you are attending. Pay close attention to it and if you notice it, don't forget to ask yourself - Is this making me more peaceful or is this taking away my peace of mind?

7. PRINCIPLE THREE: THE URGE TO SHARE

In a world dominated by instant and always-on communication, it is quite easy to develop impatience in your behavior. It can seep into your personality without you realizing it. But if peace of mind is important to you, it is essential to cultivate the ability to pause, reflect, and choose your words wisely before sharing them with others.

An urge to share refers to feeling impatient within your mind and body to express your thoughts, emotions, or opinions quickly, instantly, without considering the consequences or the potential impact on yourself and others. It often stems from a desire for validation, a need to be heard, or an instinctive reaction to a situation. You learn something and you want to instantly rush to a friend, colleague or social media to share it with others.

This usually arises from an inner compulsion you are unable to control and tends to keep you restless on an ongoing basis. It starts with a mental compulsion which quickly turns into a physical compulsion to do something - to speak or write - to share the information as quickly as possible. You might also feel a certain unease within you until you have shared it.

If you experience such an urge to share things impatiently with others, ask yourself - does that make me more peaceful or is it making me more restless?

By practicing remaining calm and patient, you can counter this urge to instantly share things with others. Taking a step back and thinking about what you are about to do provides you with an opportunity for self-reflection. You can consider if sharing impatiently is really necessary and how this impatience to share is affecting your peace of mind. When you pause before sharing, you create a space to evaluate your intentions and motivations. You can ask yourself if what you are about to share:

- aligns with your values,
- if it feels right to you,
- if it contributes positively to the conversation,
- if it is a compulsive response, and
- if it is increasing your restlessness.

If you share something that doesn't really align with your values or you don't feel right about, it may have a negative impact on your peace of mind. If it doesn't contribute positively to the conversation or worse, contributes negatively, then it might be an unnecessary waste of your energy and may not leave you very peaceful, eventually. It might also ruffle a feather or two in the outside world. If it is merely a compulsive reaction with no substance in it or something that you haven't thought through well, you might say something unnecessary or something that you shouldn't be saying. Sharing impatiently can harm you and at times also damage your relationships with people who matter to you.

If you practice taking a pause before you share things, this self-awareness allows you to make more conscious choices about what you share. It also helps you cultivate a greater sense of inner peace and genuineness in your external communication.

An excessive urge to share may also get you to speak a lot more than is necessary, which is something you should be very careful about on this journey of self-knowledge, clarity and peace of mind (see chapter on Quantity of Speech). Adding a lot of silence throughout your day is an absolute must if you wish to make any real progress in self-improvement. We have had Adios members who have specifically said that a large part of their excessive speech came from their excessive urge to prove they were right or their urge to share things impatiently. We will discuss the importance of adding regular silence to your life in more detail in a separate chapter.

Patience and restraint also allow you to consider the impact your words may have on others. By taking a moment to reflect before sharing, you can gauge how your words might be received and how they may affect the emotions of those around you. This helps you create more caring, respectful, and loving relationships with others, especially with those who matter the most to you.

By refraining from impulsive sharing, you can focus on listening, learning, and considering different viewpoints. If you are not sharing, you are silent. As I said earlier, silence is good for you. Extremely good. If you are silent, you can listen better, think better and hence develop new ideas and perspectives which can then improve how you feel about yourself.

If you wish to maintain your inner peace, it is crucial to understand the profound influence impatient sharing has on your personal well-being. Impulsively sharing information and ignoring its effect on your own peace of mind can leave you feeling restless on an ongoing basis.

For example, you have an enlightening realization about a personal challenge, but instead of taking the time to reflect and learn from it, you impulsively share it with others. Say, you have a moment of clarity about a mistake you've been making in your parenting approach. Excitedly, you mention it to a group of fellow parents without fully processing the impact or potential solutions, leading to unsolicited advice, and perhaps inviting some negative judgment from them. Or say, after an argument with your partner, you recognize a recurring pattern in their behavior. Without discussing it with them first, you instead discuss this with your friends, causing your partner to feel exposed, betrayed, and humiliated.

Instead of rushing to share it, if you took the time to think about it deeply, alone, quietly, you might learn a few things that might help you improve your long-term well-being. You might understand your mind a lot better and notice its restless nature so you know what you should or shouldn't do in the future and thus create a deeper connection with yourself. By neglecting this and instead impatiently sharing it with others, you will never get to those realizations and your thinking will remain shallow. You might sometimes gain some instant validation or satisfaction from the reactions you receive, but in the long run it might leave you feeling hollow and restless.

When you feel compelled to instantly share your thoughts, ideas, emotions, or experiences without reflecting on them first, you are unable to process and understand your own feelings because all your focus is on letting that information out to others. Cultivating patience in sharing allows you to develop a deeper connection with your inner self so you can understand what is good for your inner peace and what isn't.

Impatient sharing can also cloud your thoughts and create mental clutter. When you impulsively share your ideas, opinions, or plans without allowing yourself the time and space to gain clarity and coherence, you scatter your energy and affect your ability to articulate your views clearly. Being patient in sharing helps you think more clearly, allowing you to communicate more clearly and maintain a greater sense of peace within your own mind.

Say you are a marketing manager, and you conceive a ground-breaking marketing idea for the upcoming product release. But instead of sitting with it for some time, refining it and allowing it to crystallize within your own mind, you impatiently share it with your superiors. This might potentially dilute its potency and diminish your own sense of clarity and peace because you are more focused on instantly impressing others rather than having the patience to develop it and give it a concrete shape.

In certain instances, such a habit might also diminish your respect in the eyes of others and the confidence that they can place in you. 'She always rushes to share her half-baked ideas without having thought through them clearly' may affect the willingness of others to collaborate with you, which might be necessary to maximize your own potential and fulfillment.

Sharing impulsively can diminish your personal growth and impair your ability to learn from your experiences. When you rush to share your accomplishments, failures, or lessons without taking the time to reflect on them, you miss the valuable insights that can help you improve and move forward.

For example, you achieve a significant personal milestone at work, but instead of taking the time to reflect on the journey in silence and truly understand what this means to you going forward, you hastily share it with others to gain quick appreciation. This might potentially dilute the meaningfulness of the experience for yourself and diminish your sense of fulfillment.

A similar dilution of experience can occur if you focus too much on sharing your personal pictures or moments with the world rather than staying with them and quietly taking them in. You might miss something very beautiful and calming in the process.

Impatient sharing can also stem from a desire to feel accepted in a friendship or gain attention from colleagues or strangers. When you hastily share personal information or experiences to seek instant appreciation or to be the center of attention, you may compromise your peace of mind. For example, in a social gathering, you might impatiently share personal anecdotes, exaggerating details to seek attention from others. This impulsive need for validation might lead to temporary superficial connections but might leave a permanent sense of emptiness within you, ultimately diminishing your inner peace.

Oversharing is also something you need to be careful about. You need to know when to stop sharing information with others, especially when it is about your personal life or information that might be sensitive in nature.

Notice how various Adios principles can intertwine with each other very often in real life. For instance, in the examples we just considered, you might also experience an urge to prove, to speak too much and to focus outward more than inward. These three principles are covered in detail in their respective chapters.

Cultivating patience and the ability to hold yourself back in your communication helps a lot in making you feel more peaceful. During your Contemplation sessions, reflect on your day and recognize the moments when you felt an urge to share impulsively, and consciously decide to be careful the next time you are in such a situation. Chances are, you will be in a similar situation very soon.

Practice becoming aware of what you do and whether it makes you feel more or less peaceful, so you can control your impatience the next time. Also practice giving others the time to share without interrupting or rushing to respond to them with your own views. Speaking less in general helps in this regard because it allows you to add a good measure of silence to your life. This creates an environment for Contemplation and self-reflection, leading to a lasting sense of inner peace.

Identify when this urge to share occurs the most - does it happen in a certain environment, with specific people, in a particular state of mind, about certain topics? If you can identify it clearly, you can prepare yourself to remain aware of your behavior before you enter such situations.

The urge to share, like other urges, is similar to an addiction. If your body is unable to control itself from doing something, you have become an addict, whether that something is consumption of alcohol or drugs, or it is speaking too much, proving someone wrong, or sharing something impatiently. Controlling your urge to share will help you feel more peaceful and less restless through the day, and eventually, through your life.

In which dimensions of your life today can you apply the ADIOS principle of The Urge to Share?

_____

_____

_____

DANIELLE'S ADIOSCOPE

Situation

I discovered a secret about my best friend's husband cheating on her. I'm torn about whether to tell the truth or stay silent. I have a picture of him in an intimate embrace with another woman and I want to post that picture on social media to expose his infidelity. This could destroy their marriage and our friendship. But hiding it also eats away at me.

Twin Voices:

I hear two distinct voices within me. Let's call them the voice of the heart and the voice of the head.

Voice 1, the voice of the heart, urges me to expose the truth. It insists that my best friend, Naomi, deserves to know the reality of her husband's betrayal. It argues that by sharing the picture online, I can free her from a deceptive marriage and protect her from future heartache. The voice tells me that loyalty and honesty is more important.

Voice 2, the voice of logic, asks me to be careful. It warns that sharing this secret could really hurt Naomi. It could damage her emotions, her marriage, her other relationships, and our friendship. This voice says it's not my place to get involved in her personal life. I need to think about how my actions could impact everything, and not get intoxicated by the desire to be my friend's savior.

The Urge to Share

Does this make you more restless or more peaceful?

If I hastily share the picture, I will get an instant high of having done something very grand, having saved my friend's life from a monster husband. While that temptation is quite strong, it does not align well with my values. Exposing personal matters on a public platform doesn't make me comfortable. While the picture of James cheating on Naomi is troubling me, this urge to share it publicly is making me even more restless. This could also hurt Naomi and harm our relationship and the trust we have shared for many years.

JAMIE'S ADIOSCOPE:

Situation

I share my pregnancy news online too frequently, which is leading to problems in my marriage. At first, I was so excited and wanted everyone to know. But now tensions are growing between my husband and me. We have started arguing more and are growing distant. Social media has become a barrier between us. By making our personal life public, even when he wanted me to keep it private, I opened both of us to unwanted opinions and judgment. Our struggles are now displayed for all to comment on, and it is damaging our relationship.

The Urge to Prove:

When I reflect on my current situation, I realize that I have been trying to prove myself right and my husband wrong. For example, during a recent argument about whether we should send our child to a regular school or choose to homeschool, I insisted on my way of doing things without even considering his perspective or hearing him out completely. This came from my personal experiences during my boarding school days. As if that wasn't enough, in the heat of the moment, I also posted our discussion on social media. What was I thinking! This not only enraged him, but I felt terrible about it myself later on. It left me feeling more restless and disconnected from him.

Another time, when someone on social media disagreed with my decision to post pregnancy updates and suggested that I shouldn't do it, I felt the need to defend my actions and prove that I was right in sharing those moments. This constant need for validation and proving myself has only added to my restlessness and insecurity.

By constantly trying to prove myself right or others wrong, I have created a barrier between myself and those around me, most importantly my husband, who means the world to me. I need to add some silence to my life and pay more attention to what I say and how I say it.

The Urge to Share:

I often shared personal details on social media without reflecting on the consequences. For example, I definitely shouldn't have posted our schooling discussion online. It was a private conversation with my husband, but I constantly feel this urge to let everyone know what is happening in my life.

People are building their business in public nowadays, but maybe building a baby in public is not such a good idea. It is a much more private, intimate affair. This instant sharing without careful consideration also often leads to negative comments and judgment, leaving me feeling restless and stressed when I go to bed. Instead of enjoying my motherhood, I often lay awake at night thinking about all the judgment I receive and sometimes cry myself to sleep. Stress is not good for my baby.

Also, once I also shared my premature and not very pleasant opinion on certain pregnancy foods that another parent was eating. That drew a lot of flak and I realized I was trying to be clever and outsmart others.

All this has also increased the emotional distance between my husband and I, which is constantly chipping away my peace of mind.

I need to quietly focus on our bond and love that we still share (hopefully!), rather than invite the outside world into our bedroom. I will feel peaceful only when we share a close, happy relationship. Some social opinions might feel good in the moment, but they are meaningless in the long run. At times, they don't even feel good in the moment because there is just so much negativity and judgment being thrown at you. In all of this, I am losing something much more important to me. Not worth it.

CHAPTER TAKEAWAYS:

- If you experience an urge to impatiently share things with others, ask yourself how it makes you feel - does it make you more restless?
- Speaking less in general can help you control such an urge. Adding silence also helps you think and reflect better and share only what is really necessary.
- Excessive sharing can also invite negative judgment from others, which might make you more restless and stressed.
- You might be tempted to impatiently share ideas, emotions, or experiences with others, or exaggerate yourself to gain short-term attention, but it might eventually leave you feeling more restless.

8. PRINCIPLE FOUR: THOUGHT ACTION LINKAGE

Every action you take starts with a thought. Whether it's a simple decision, a conversation with someone, or a new endeavor, it all begins in your mind. By gaining a deeper understanding of your thoughts and learning to change them when necessary, you can change your actions and hence change how you feel within.

It's not just about thinking; it's about analyzing your thoughts, gaining an insight into your mind, and becoming the scientist of your own thoughts. Imagine putting all your thoughts on a table, observing them with a curious and analytical mindset. By doing so, you will understand your mind better. That will help you make better choices which then lead to a more fulfilling, purposeful and peaceful life.

To truly understand your thoughts, you must spend quality time with them. Just as you need to spend time with someone to get to know them better, you need to dedicate time to analyzing your own thoughts—alone. This regular introspection will help you understand your mind well so you can use it in the right manner rather than being on autopilot and letting it use you.

Changing your thoughts is not easy; it requires time, patience and practice. However, the rewards that come with this practice are immense. By consciously changing your thoughts, you can transform your actions and create a life filled with purpose and inner peace.

THE LINK BETWEEN YOUR THOUGHTS AND ACTIONS

You have a constant stream of thoughts flowing through your mind. These thoughts have a profound impact on your behavior and the choices you make. Every action you take, whether big or small, starts with a thought.

Have you ever noticed how your thoughts can influence your behavior? When you have positive and optimistic thoughts, you tend to approach situations with enthusiasm and take proactive steps toward achieving your goals. You also tend to feel more fulfilled and peaceful in such situations. On the other hand, negative thoughts can hold you back, creating doubt and fear that prevent you from acting, or can encourage you to take wrong actions that you might later regret and hence reduce your overall peace of mind.

Think of thoughts as people, real people who can influence what you do. Imagine a simple situation where a few good friends of yours are insisting that you stay longer at a party: "Come on, stay for some more time. We all are here. What's the rush to go back home so soon?" In many situations, it is likely that you will agree and stay back and never think about it.

But now I want you to think about it. Think about what just happened. You allowed yourself to get influenced by your friends and decided. Now imagine that another group of friends is insisting that you do something immoral, or unhealthy. In some situations, you might agree to that as well. That is because our friends can have a real influence on us, especially if your own inner voice isn't strong enough to counter that influence.

Similarly, you could also be influenced by a public figure you may have never met in person but what they say or do might resonate strongly with you and influence you to take certain actions, good or bad. Think of leaders who have inspired people to do something inspiring and worthwhile, and also leaders who have provoked people to do something unhealthy and terrible.

Your thoughts are similar to such influential friends or public figures. Just like you might be influenced by what they are saying and take some action, you are also influenced by what your thoughts are saying and take some action, good or bad, right, or wrong, harmful or harmless. By recognizing the link between your thoughts and actions, you gain a powerful tool that can help you take the right actions and hence to create a life that is fulfilling, that focuses on long term inner peace rather than short term excitement or restlessness.

Think about a few actions you've taken or decisions you've made recently or in the past. These were your final actions. Now, can you identify the thoughts that preceded those actions? Were they coming from an inner sense of peace, or did they stem from self-doubt, fear, anger or some other negative emotion? Did you say something unpleasant to your mother or father or sibling because you were rehearsing it in your mind for too long? Did you not do something you know you should have done because you kept telling yourself that you can't do it? Did you do some-thing you knew was wrong, but you did it anyway because external influence was dominating your thoughts?

Understanding the connection between your thoughts and actions requires regular Contemplation. Take the time to observe your thoughts and identify any recurring themes or tendencies. Notice how certain thoughts lead to specific actions and outcomes. You can't do this if you don't pause and focus on it specifically. Thoughts are way too subtle, and they are absolutely silent. So, it is very easy to miss them unless you pay specific attention. If you keep going about your life focusing on the external world, your busyness may never let you see your thoughts. Your mind can be quite a trickster.

As you pay attention to your thoughts for a few days, you will start to see how powerful they are and how they can influence your actions, sometimes even negatively, if you aren't paying attention. You will discover that by consciously choosing thoughts that are aligned with making you feel fulfilled, purposeful, and peaceful, you can ensure your actions are in the same direction as well.

An example of how your thoughts influence your actions could be during an argument with a loved one. When you're in a fight with someone you love, your thoughts affect how you act. If you just think about wanting to hurt them back, you might say mean things. But if you stop and understand that your thoughts can make you act in an unhealthy manner, you can do better. Instead of hurting them, you could tell them how you feel calmly. Then you can work on finding a solution together. Your thoughts have power over your actions. Being aware of them helps you make better choices.

You can choose the thoughts you hold about the people in your life. Instead of focusing on their flaws or shortcomings, think about their positive attributes and appreciate the qualities that they have but you don't. Someone might not be as financially successful as you are, but might be more care-giving and loving. Someone might be more talkative, but also have a more honest heart. Someone might be more insecure, but also more supportive when the going gets tough.

Focusing on someone's flaws can be extremely rewarding to the ego and can come very naturally, but that's where you need to remind yourself that your mind doesn't always act in a manner that makes you more peaceful. The loudest voice in your head is not necessarily the right one. You need to choose the voice you wish to follow rather than be bullied by the loudest voice in your head.

Wrong thoughts can damage your relationships so pay attention to any negative thoughts that may arise in your relationships and push them back consciously. Your smile is a very powerful antidote to negative thoughts. Use it often. Saying "thank you" thoughtfully, by feeling it inside of you and not just saying it mechanically, can also help you defuse negative thoughts about the other person. Genuine appreciation strengthens bonds and builds a deeper sense of connection. Eliminating negative thoughts and replacing them with positive ones will significantly reduce the possibility of taking a negative action that might take away your peace of mind and also damage your relationship with a loved one.

This negotiation with negative thoughts and replacing them with positive ones is an ongoing exercise. You might lose the battle off and on but if you keep at it, you will keep getting better and better. The goal is to keep moving forward. A saint is a sinner who never stopped practicing. Contemplation on an earlier situation where you lost control is a good exercise because it helps you analyze what happened and what you could have done but did not do in that situation which resulted in an action that reduced your peace of mind. As you keep working on this, you will slowly develop new muscle memory which will discourage negative thoughts the moment they arise and encourage positive thoughts which will help you do or say the things that bring more fulfillment and inner peace.

Your thoughts also play a vital role in shaping your mindset, attitude, and overall success in the workplace. If you are careful about the thoughts that are driving your career, you will be better able to maximize your potential and do what you were meant to do. You will be able to create better professional relationships and a more fulfilling and meaningful work experience. You might spend many hours a week at work, so pay attention to how your thoughts are affecting your peace of mind at work.

For example, if your thoughts are around imitating what others are doing rather than looking within to find what work is more meaningful for you, you might end up choosing the wrong line of work or a wrong organization. If you are feeling stressed and overwhelmed and your thoughts are constantly centered on self-doubt and negativity, your actions may be to procrastinate or avoid a task altogether. But if you understand your mind well using Contemplation, you will understand why you feel self-doubt. By using the principles in this book, you will be able to think more clearly about your work and find motivation for it.

Most people don't find the work that is right for them, the work that will make them feel fulfilled, the work that will give meaning to their life, the work that will make them peaceful. That's because they don't take the time to think deeply about it but go about their life in an autopilot mode. Some people find something that they want to do. Some people find something that they like to do. But very few people find something that they have to do. Something that they were born to do. Contemplation will help you find that.

The priorities in your Vision Planner might help you think more clearly in this regard. If you are clear about what will make you feel more fulfilled, purposeful, and peaceful, it becomes easier to focus on tasks that help you move in that direction. Also don't forget to plan your actions in accordance with your Adios year (your birthday to birthday) and break them down into Adios quarters and months. That can keep things more relevant and relatable to you.

MICHAEL'S ADIOSCOPE

Situation

I got really angry and blew up at my partner for not helping with chores. I let my frustration take over and accused him of being lazy and selfish. I didn't listen and turned a discussion into a bad fight. Now he's upset and I'm eating dinner alone. I need to control my anger better next time.

Twin Voices:

Voice 1: I should have an open and honest but polite conversation with Jason, expressing how overwhelmed I feel with the household chores. I'm sure he will understand because we love each other. Discuss the division of responsibilities together and find a compromise that works for both of us.

Voice 2: Instead of confronting him, take the initiative to complete the tasks together and make it a bonding experience. Show understanding and support for his busy schedule while gently encouraging him to contribute.

Voice 3: Consider hiring a cleaning service or outsourcing some of the chores. This way, both of us can focus on other aspects of our lives without the added stress of household responsibilities.

In the long run, following a combination of Voice 1 and 2 would likely bring more peace. By having an open conversation and most importantly in a friendly manner, I can express my feelings and concerns while also understanding Jason's perspective. Through dialogue, we can work toward distributing the household chores, and maintain our love and mutual respect. Maybe we could bring in a cleaning service once in a while as well for a change. It is expensive so we may not be able to afford it every week.

The urge to prove:

I realize that I have been trying to prove my point and make Jason understand that he should do more around the house. I have been too focused on proving him wrong and highlighting his laziness and it has only fueled my anger and restlessness. I often find myself replaying this conversation in my mind and thinking of how I will confront and accuse him, what I will say, mostly at bedtime but also sometimes when I am at work.

This urge to prove myself right has created a hostile atmosphere, pushing us further apart instead of finding a solution. There has been an undercurrent of tension even when we sit down for dinner together. Yes, I ask him 'Hey, are you okay?' and he says 'Yes', but I know that's not true. And it's all my doing.

Thought Action Linkage:

I realize that my frustration at having to handle all the household chores alone has led to this anger for Jason. These negative thoughts dictate my actions, pushing me into that heated argument with him.

I need to be vigilant about my thoughts. When I start feeling the frustration bubble up again about Jason and the chores, I will pause and remind myself that he has his own set of responsibilities. I need to remember that the way to address this issue is through calm and respectful discussion, not heated confrontation.

When we start arguing, profanity very quickly finds a way into our speech and gradually the pitch and volume of our speech rise until there is an explosion, followed by a deafening silence. After that, a heavy air of toxicity hangs above us for a few days. This takes away all my peace of mind. So I need to watch my thoughts and also what I say and how I say it. Also the next time I catch myself rehearsing the argument in my mind, I will stop right there.

ROBERT'S ADIOSCOPE:

Situation

I've been feeling jealous of my friend's success lately. He seems to be achieving so much while I compare myself and feel inadequate. When I confessed feeling envious, my friend said he admires my drive, and we all have our own paths. His words were comforting but didn't make the envy go away fully. At a party at his fancy new house the other day, I heard others wishing for what he has. That made me realize I'm not alone in feeling this way, but focusing on others holds me back. I need to overcome this on my own and pursue my dreams, rather than envy him.

Twin Voices:

Voice 1: Acknowledge your feelings of envy and use them as motivation to work harder and get ahead of him. It's okay to feel envious, but don't let it consume you. Instead, let it fuel your determination.

Voice 2: Focus on your own journey and be thankful for the accomplishments you've already achieved. You have your own unique personality, strengths and what brings you fulfillment and peace of mind. Stop comparing yourself to Alex and remember that everyone's path to success is different. Be genuinely happy for his success but find your own path.

The first voice is very tempting because it excites me to work harder, but I notice that it leaves me less peaceful deep down. I might succeed but may still not be very peaceful because I will still be looking at Alex and comparing myself to him to ensure I am more successful than him. My focus will always be on him, on the outside.

In the long run, following Voice 2 would bring me more peace. By focusing on my own journey, I can be true to who I am and what makes me more fulfilled. When I am at peace with my life, I will also be able to genuinely appreciate my friend's success, which is the right thing to do and that will make me feel more peaceful. He is an old buddy of mine, and I certainly don't wish to dent our friendship.

Thought Action Linkage:

The thought action linkage has been a powerful force in my life, especially regarding my envious thoughts about Alex. Whenever I compare my achievements to his, I notice how these thoughts directly affect my actions and overall well-being.

For example, when Alex landed his high-paying job and bought a new house, instead of feeling genuinely happy for him, my envy crept in, making me feel inadequate. These negative thoughts kept circulating inside my head and paralyzed me. Instead of exploring opportunities to move forward that could have helped me succeed in my own endeavors, I spent a lot of time brooding about Alex's success. I was also sarcastic with him at one or two instances. So my thoughts led to two things - me not doing anything about my own progress and constantly feeling bad about his success.

These envious thoughts have been affecting my professional life as well. Whenever a colleague receives recognition or promotion, my mind immediately drifts into thoughts of comparison. Instead of using their success as inspiration to push myself further, I feel demotivated and question my own abilities.

I now realize that by continuously thinking negatively, I am sabotaging my own potential for growth and success. I have multiple voices in my mind. Those are my thoughts. I need to be careful about the voice I repeat in my mind constantly, because that voice then dominates my mind and hence my actions.

(Edit: Four days later) To break free from this negative cycle, I have started to actively challenge and reframe my envious thoughts. When I catch myself feeling jealous of someone's accomplishments, I remind myself that their journey is unique, and mine will unfold in its own time. I want to focus on my strengths and what makes me feel more fulfilled. I have started spending time thinking about what will make me feel more fulfilled, what kind of work will I find meaningful, something I can resonate with.

It's not easy, and I still face moments of envy occasionally. However, I am determined to stay conscious of my thoughts and not let my negative voice overpower my mind.

CHAPTER TAKEAWAYS:

- Every action starts with a thought. If you allow wrong thoughts to persist in your mind, you will tend to take wrong actions.
- Thoughts are similar to influential friends or public figures. They have the ability to persuade you and get you to do or say things they want you to do or say. So be careful about the thoughts you repeat in your mind.
- Sometimes, repeating an angry or fearful thought ensures that you will take an angry or fearful action. Choose your thoughts wisely.

～

9. PRINCIPLE FIVE: RIGHT VS WRONG

When it comes to making choices in life, whether at home or outside, you need to determine what is right and what is wrong. But how do you do that?

You might have to decide between doing or not doing something a friend has suggested, to go or not go to a party, to eat this or not, to wear this or not, to buy this home or not, to live in this neighborhood or not, to work at this company or not, to marry or not, to marry this person or not, to have a child or not, to have another child or not, to agree to doing chemotherapy for your parent or not, to donate to this foundation or not, to focus on money or the vision.

What is right and what is wrong? How do you decide? The answer to this question lies within your own peace of mind. Here is how we will define right and wrong as per Adios:

Anything that decreases your peace of mind or increases your restlessness is wrong for you. Anything that increases your peace of mind or reduces your restlessness is right for you.

To truly understand and define right and wrong, you must become intimately acquainted with your inner self. Take a moment to think about the choices you've made in the past. How did they affect your peace of mind? Did they bring you contentment and calmness or leave you feeling unsettled and restless?

We are not talking about happiness. We are talking about peace of mind. Peace of mind is not a fleeting sensation of pleasure or excitement. We are referring to a feeling of contentment and peace that lasts for a long time. Happiness is good to have too, but it is important to understand the difference between happiness and peace of mind. Happiness can be short-lived sometimes, and in some cases can even go against your long-term peace of mind. Do not mistake happiness for peace of mind every time.

To choose wisely, you must be familiar with your own feelings. Pay attention to how certain choices make you feel. Does a particular decision bring you a sense of calm and clarity, or does it stir up unease and turmoil within you? Your feelings are powerful indicators, serving as signposts on the path toward making choices that will maintain your inner peace.

Think back to a time when you made a decision that went against your instincts, against what felt right in your heart. How did that affect your peace of mind? Did it create inner conflict? Understanding the impact of your choice on your peace of mind can help you make the right choice.

The essence of right and wrong lies within you. It is not determined by external factors. Trust yourself and your inner compass. The test is simple - will this make me peaceful, or will this take away my peace of mind?

As you read further, think about the power of Contemplation in this regard. By thinking deeply about what is right or wrong for you - what makes you more or less peaceful, you will be able to create and maintain a more fulfilling, purposeful, and peaceful life.

How have your past choices impacted your peace of mind at home or at work? What insights have you gained from your past decisions? To define your moral compass clearly, you need to start with understanding the sense of right and wrong within you.

Whether it's a disagreement with a friend, a conflict with a family member, or a challenging situation with a colleague, the way you handle these interactions can impact your peace of mind, sometimes for a very long time. When faced with a disagreement, pause and reflect on how your words or actions might affect your peace of mind as well as the relationship. Will your response make things more peaceful, or will it escalate tensions? By choosing to communicate thoughtfully, you can maintain your own peace of mind and also create healthier relationships with others.

Your decisions about your work can be very critical for your long-term well-being. Whether you're deciding on a job, considering a promotion, or planning to start on your own, it's essential to evaluate how these choices align with your values and long-term peace of mind. Ask yourself: Will this path bring me a sense of fulfillment and satisfaction? Does it resonate with my core beliefs or am I only being attracted to the money or other such factors? By selecting a career that aligns with your long-term well-being, you can find greater meaning and joy in your work, leading to a more peaceful and purposeful work life.

In every dimension of life, the choice between right and wrong ultimately comes down to what makes you more peaceful vs what makes you less peaceful or more restless. Use the practice of Contemplation to listen to the various voices inside of you carefully and assess their impact on your peace of mind. When faced with decisions, take a moment to sit in silence or go for a Contemplation walk, think deeply, and choose the option that will bring you long term inner peace. Some choices might offer short-term excitement and can be quite tempting. Focus on choices that improve and maintain your peace of mind, so you can create a more fulfilling and peaceful life.

Analyze your old decisions in your personal or professional life. How did they impact your peace of mind? What lessons have you learned? Is there something you are dealing with right now where you should choose to do what makes you more peaceful rather than choose the other voice that is much louder but may not make you peaceful in the long run?

The words you choose and how you express yourself greatly impact your relationships and your own sense of peace. Pay attention to situations where you must decide between speaking truthfully or lying, between constructive criticism or hurtful remarks, and between speaking less or speaking too much. By choosing thoughtful, respectful, and moderate communication, you might feel more peaceful.

Imagine a work meeting where a colleague presents an idea that differs from your own. You can choose to listen attentively, express your opinions with respect, and engage in a productive discussion. By doing so, you might promote a harmonious work environment and maintain your own peace of mind. By inter-rupting them constantly and speaking in a sarcastic tone, you might reduce your peace of mind and also hurt your relationship with others.

Taking care of yourself is crucial for maintaining inner peace. Consider situations where you must choose between taking care of your mind and body or neglecting your well-being for the sake of unimportant external demands.

Let's say you are having a busy day where you have multiple commitments, but you also feel exhausted and in need of rest. You have the choice to push yourself beyond your limits or take a break and relax or engage in a hobby you enjoy. Binge-watching a series on the internet every evening might provide instant pleasure, but you may also lose many productive hours or disturb your sleep cycle. What would make you more peaceful? Ask yourself and decide accordingly.

Raising a child can involve numerous choices where you must choose between right and wrong. So many that in certain cases you might feel overwhelmed. By consciously considering the impact of your decisions on your child's well-being and your own peace of mind, you can navigate the challenges of parenting in a way that maintains overall peace and well-being at home and builds a strong bond with your child. Embodying stillness, a habit of self-reflection and an approach that always focuses on peace of mind as the desired outcome will help you create the right environment at home.

If you inspire your child to become introspective and contemplative by being such a person yourself, it will help them deal with many other problems or questions they face in their life confidently on their own without getting unduly influenced by others. They may never share some of these problems with you. In many of those instances, they could make a decision so wrong that could turn their life in a dangerous direction.

It is during such moments that their own inner moral compass, their own contemplative nature and their ability to differentiate between right and wrong will help them make the right choice, even if their peers are insisting that they choose the wrong option. Contemplation not only provides you with clarity of thought but also gives you the courage to make the right choice, the choice that makes you more peaceful, even if that choice is not the most popular one.

The best way to help your child is to embody those qualities yourself on a daily basis. By training yourself to be more calm, contemplative and peaceful, you create the right positive environment at home that is then naturally imbibed by your children. When they see you making the right choices calmly day in and day out, at home, at the dinner table, at a social event, at a supermarket, at a family gathering, etc., you are indirectly training them to be calm and peaceful through each of those actions of yours.

Sometimes as a parent you might feel that despite maintaining such an environment at home, you don't seem to be making a difference in your child's life. You might start to wonder whether it is even useful to do so and might think of giving up. Please rest assured that if you are really maintaining a contemplative and peaceful environment at home on a regular basis by being such a person yourself, even though your child may not fully imbibe those qualities or sometimes might even rebel at it, your work is not going waste. It is building a foundation inside your child. The right foundation.

When they experience the restlessness of the external world in the next few years and feel the stress, this foundational work that you have done for so many years will then become meaningful to them, and they will eventually seek it and return to it. But if you give up your efforts today, what will they return to? The only option for them would be that stressful, restless external world.

It might take 20 or 30 years for them to realize it, but once they do, at least they will have something to return to where they can feel peaceful. They need to live their own life. They need to discover their own peace. No matter how much you know what is right for them, they still need to feel it themselves, discover it on their own. Once they experience the restless world outside, they will then remember the contemplative and peaceful world that you had taught them to build. Sometimes, it is important to experience the darkness to fully appreciate the light.

Your role as a parent is to work tirelessly, for years, to build that right foundation in their mind, quietly, without complaining, and without expecting anything. If you do that, I assure you. Your work will never go to waste. Never.

Do the right thing because it is the right thing to do. There is no better reason to do it.

In your everyday life, you may encounter other situations where you must decide between right and wrong. It could be as simple as finding a lost wallet and choosing to return it to its rightful owner, or as complex as standing up against injustice in your community.

For instance, imagine you witness someone being bullied at school. You have the power to decide whether to remain silent and ignore the situation or to intervene and stand up for what is right. You may have your own reasons to do either, but only you can decide what is right for you, what makes you more peaceful.

Just because standing up sounds impressive doesn't mean it is right for you every time.

Just because breaking up sounds terrible doesn't mean it is wrong for you every time.

You may encounter situations where your friends or peers encourage you to engage in activities that go against your values or beliefs. You might be torn between keeping them happy and remaining peaceful internally. It can be challenging to resist peer pressure, especially if you don't have a strong connection with yourself. You might feel tempted to do as they say to avoid feeling left out or judged. But tell yourself - whatever makes me more peaceful is right for me and whatever makes me less peaceful or more restless is wrong for me. Say it aloud to yourself.

Your true friends will respect you for your choices, even if they differ from theirs. And if they don't, it might be time to change your friends, not your choices.

If you are looking for a partner, choosing someone merely to get rid of your loneliness quickly, or due to peer pressure or on the basis of some superficial factors might provide some satisfaction in the short run, but may not work out very well in the long run. If you don't ask yourself - what will make me more peaceful and fulfilled in the long run - you will never know yourself well. If you don't know yourself well, how will you know who you should be with and why?

If you don't know yourself deeply, then you know yourself only at a shallow level. Shallowness usually lets you down. It believes in things that make you feel good in the moment. Don't fall into that trap.

Find yourself first before you find a partner. Know clearly being with what kind of a person will make you feel more peaceful. Also know the qualities in a person that might reduce your peace of mind, so you don't fall for the wrong person. If some of these negative qualities are deal breakers, do not let other superficial positive qualities charm you into ignoring the red flags in someone's personality. A financially successful partner who doesn't respect you might not bring you peace of mind.

If you both are not aligned at a fundamental level, at the level of your values and what will make you feel fulfilled and peaceful in the long run, then short-term physical intimacy, fancy dinners, and exciting getaways won't be enough to create a healthy long-term relationship. If you can't connect with the soul of your partner, connecting with their body might last only for a short while.

If you aren't clear from within, if you haven't found yourself yet, no sophisticated AI algorithm on a dating site can help you find the right person. The algorithm will take what you have written in your profile as true, but if you don't really know what makes you more peaceful in the long run, you may not have written the right things in your profile. An algorithm can't help you in that case.

Similarly, letting go of someone because it isn't working out can be very hard. Sometimes not making it work has the sound of failure. But do what makes you feel more peaceful in the long run. Don't do it in a hurry. Take your time so your decision isn't rushed or impulsive. But if you are sure, it is time to let go because it will make you more peaceful, then do it. Even after you let go physically, you also need to let go of them mentally, so your shoulders and mind feel lighter. Ask the same question again - what will make me feel more peaceful? Your lightness is crucial so you can start your new life with a smile.

Find yourself first. Be clear about what makes you feel fulfilled and peaceful. You will gain this clarity through Contemplation.

As a leader, you will be faced with countless situations where you need to choose between right and wrong. Many choices might be tempting, some even forcing you to do something to please others, or to prove something, rather than being true to who you really are, your own values and vision. Don't lose your focus. Remind yourself - whatever makes me more peaceful is right for me; whatever makes me less peaceful is wrong for me.

Speak to other people in the Adios community. How they made the right choices in their relationships, work, parenting and other dimensions will also give you the clarity, courage, inspiration and strength to make the right choice yourself. Some choices can make or break you. You must know how to make the right one.

The choices you make in various dimensions of your life have a direct impact on your peace of mind. By consciously considering how your decisions will make you feel, you can create a more peaceful and fulfilling life.

As you go about your day, use Contemplation to listen to your inner voices and choose the one that makes you more peaceful. Trust yourself and your ability to make choices that prioritize your peace of mind. Just because many others are choosing something else doesn't mean that is right for you. It may not even be right for them, but they may not have thought about it deeply. A unanimous decision is just a unanimous decision. It is not necessarily the right decision.

Make your decisions wisely. Whatever makes you less peaceful is wrong for you. Whatever makes you more peaceful is right for you.

In which dimensions of your life today can you apply the ADIOS principle of Right vs Wrong?

_____

_____

_____

SARAH'S ADIOSCOPE

Situation

I have to decide between choosing Tom and Julia to lead an important project, but I just can't make up my mind. Tom has a solid track record, while Julia brings fresh ideas. They're both great candidates, and I know they have a lot to offer.

Twin Voices:

Voice 1 says: Hire Tom for the team. He has proven reliability, a strong track record, and extensive experience with the company.

Voice 2 says: Hire Julia for the team. She is a rising star, a natural leader with fresh ideas, and brings a new perspective to the project.

To determine which voice would make me more peaceful in the long run, I need to understand how each option impacts the success of the project. I need to consider how Tom's and Julia's strengths fit the needs of the team and the project's goals. While both of them fit well, does one of them fit much better given our current challenges? Additionally, I have to consider their ability to handle the team well.

Right vs Wrong (more vs less peaceful)

While Tom is more experienced, Julia is a better leader and can bring everyone together as a team and rally them toward a cause. Tom cannot do that. She also knows her values strongly. Tom is more of a loner and an excellent individual contributor.

So though it initially felt like I had to choose between experience and fresh ideas, I now see a completely new dimension in this situation. Now I feel a sense of satisfaction and peace thinking about Julia as the leader with Tom in a senior supporting role in the project. I also feel confident of explaining this reasoning to Tom and I'm sure he will agree with me and understand where I am coming from. Both of them care about the project, but to lead it, we need someone who also has better leadership skills. This choice feels right to me. It certainly makes me peaceful within.

JENNIFER'S ADIOSCOPE

Situation

My boyfriend loves me a lot, but when he gets angry, he loses his temper to the extent that he beats me sometimes. He always comes around and apologizes profusely but then it happens again. And again. We are four days away from our wedding. The invites have gone out. The venue has been booked and paid for. Today, over an insignificant disagreement, he hit me again. But today was the worst of all. He kicked me on the face with his foot. With his shoes on. I now have scars on my face. The wedding is in four days.

Twin Voices

Voice 1 - Leave him. Forget about the invites or the venue. That is money already spent. You still have a chance to not spend yourself.

Voice 2 - He loves me. I love him. I think my love as a wife and the mother of our children will change him after the wedding.

In my Voice 1, I also hear many of my friends. But I think he will change after our marriage. He came back in the morning and was crying like a baby. But for the first time, he said 'Baby I need help. I think I need therapy. I don't know what comes upon me.' I think I should give this a chance.

Right vs Wrong

Voice 1 is the voice of my head and it sounds logically correct. But Voice 2 makes me feel more peaceful. I feel insecure even thinking about being alone, without him in my life. Every couple has their challenges. Now that he has admitted he is open to therapy, I see hope. He will change. I will go ahead with the wedding.

(Edit: 6 days later) We are on our honeymoon. It happened again. What have I done! Why did I not walk away? Why did I not listen to the voice of my heart? Why does walking away from something toxic feel like failure, when it should feel like freedom?

DIANE'S ADIOSCOPE

Situation

I discovered unethical practices at my respected tech job. I saw secret documents showing this. Now I have to decide what to do. Should I tell people or stay quiet? Blowing the whistle could bring justice but also big risks. Not saying anything means hiding the truth. Either way, it will change my life. I'm stuck at a crossroads, not sure which path is right.

TWIN VOICES:

Voice 1 says: Expose the truth and hold the company accountable for its unethical practices. By revealing the information, I can bring about change and justice.

Voice 2 says: Stay silent and continue working, avoiding any potential risks or consequences. It suggests that maintaining the status quo will ensure stability and security.

Voice 3 says: Leave the company quietly without exposing its practices. By distancing myself from the situation and finding a new job, I can get on with my life.

Voice 4 says: Leave the company and then expose it once you find a new job. That might save the awkwardness I might go through if I were to do it while being in the company.

Right vs Wrong:

This isn't an easy one. But I do know that Voice 2 is definitely not an option. After knowing the truth about my company, I cannot continue to work here by turning a blind eye to what is really going on here.

Voice 1 feels like the right thing to do. I really want to do it, but I need to ensure that this isn't driven by excitement or an urge to prove others wrong or gain external validation by projecting myself as the hero who saved the day. It is also possible that I have misjudged the situation and am exaggerating it in my mind with my limited knowledge about the matter. I don't want to be that immature employee who made a big deal about something she didn't understand and embarrass myself later on.

Voice 3 feels like I will be running away from the situation. That might temporarily solve the problem, but I think it won't give me a long-term resolution. It will not make me peaceful and I will keep thinking about it.

I am also worried that going against a powerful organization might mean putting my career, reputation, and personal safety at risk. The potential backlash from the company, its influential allies, and even the public could be severe. Would I be hailed as a hero, exposing the truth and forcing the company to change its ways? Or would I become a target myself, facing termination, legal battles, and social isolation?

The best option right now is to dig deeper into the matter at hand and ensure that I am not overreacting or misjudging the issue. I should seek external guidance from someone senior and experienced but not part of the company who might be better able to judge the seriousness of the matter and also advise me on the potential consequences of my actions. I can then make an informed decision.

DR. RONALD HARRISON'S ADIOSCOPE

Situation

I manage doctors at a hospital that pushes us constantly to boost revenue, even via unneeded care. They want me to recommend unnecessary surgeries, redundant tests. This clashes with my ethics. I assure my team their jobs are safe, but that deepens my guilt. I'm compromising myself to keep them afloat. Suggesting alternatives to the hospital owners haven't worked. My once-noble career feels tainted. My profession is no longer just about saving lives; it's become a trade. I'm now just a cog in a profit machine.

Twin Voices:

Voice 1, the voice of my head, tells me to comply with the owner's demands. It argues that by upselling tests and surgeries, I can ensure financial security for myself, my kids and my team. I can buy a bigger house and send my kids to an expensive school. Voice 2, my heart, is my moral compass. It urges me to stand by my ethical obligations as a doctor and oppose the owner's directives, even at the risk of financial instability.

Following Voice 2, the voice of my heart, would make me more peaceful in the long run. By upholding the integrity and principles that define my profession, I would be able to look back on my career with pride, knowing that I stood my ground for what is right. Though it may not guarantee financial gain in the short term, the peace of mind and self-respect it would bring are invaluable. And it isn't as if I cannot make sufficient money by being ethical. I am an experienced and competent doctor after all. I should look for an ethical hospital to work at.

Right vs Wrong (more vs less peaceful)

Complying with the demands to upsell unneeded procedures makes me more restless. Just yesterday, to an 80-year-old woman who complained of double vision, I prescribed a tonic knowing fairly well that it won't really do much good just so she can come back in a week and I can then prescribe her an expensive procedure. I know a pill that would have solved her problem in about two weeks. My conscience is in turmoil as I feel that I'm betraying my ethical responsibilities as a doctor. Thinking about any possible legal consequences makes me even more nervous. What am I doing!!

Taking a stand against the owner's unethical directives would make me more peaceful. I became a doctor to benefit the patients, not the hospitals.

It will give me long-lasting peace of mind knowing that I've remained true to my core principles and my Hippocratic Oath. While the financial aspects are important, my inner peace is more important for me.

CHAPTER TAKEAWAYS:

- Whatever increases your peace of mind is right for you. Whatever decreases your peace of mind or increases your restlessness is wrong for you.
- Apply the filter of more peaceful vs less peaceful in your personal relationships, work, parenting and other important dimensions in your life.
- Differentiate between short-term happiness and long-term peace of mind.
- In a crucial decision, ask yourself - what will make me more peaceful and what will reduce my peace of mind?

$\sim$

10. PRINCIPLE SIX: NEGATIVE COMPARISON

Have you ever compared yourself to someone else and felt bad about yourself? Maybe it was a friend who got better grades, a colleague who was more successful, or a cousin who was more good looking. Negative comparison can make you feel inferior and unhappy.

Negative comparison happens when you look at others, think they are better than you and that makes you feel inferior or less than. You might compare your appearance, talents, or achievements to theirs. This comparison can make you feel sad, less confident, and even jealous.

The problem with negative comparison is that it focuses on what you lack instead of focusing on your own strengths and unique qualities. It can make you forget about your own accomplishments and the things that make you you. It can make you forget your own story and focus too much on someone else's. It can make you forget who you are and focus on trying to be someone else. When you constantly compare yourself to others, it's hard to feel happy and content.

Negative comparisons can happen in different areas of your life, such as school, relationships, hobbies, work, parenting and can happen in person or online. You might see someone posting pictures of their recent vacation or parties and start comparing it to your own experiences. This comparison can make you feel like your life isn't as exciting or enjoyable. You might look at the media attention another business owner gets and feel you are missing out. You might look at someone else getting the awards and start to believe you are not good enough.

Everyone has their own journey and strengths. Everyone has their own story. You are on your own path and comparing yourself to others won't bring you peace of mind. Instead of focusing on what others have, focus on what makes you feel more fulfilled, purposeful and peaceful. That's your story. Live your story.

You are you. You don't need to compare yourself to others to feel good or bad about yourself. You just need to find yourself - know yourself deeply so you can appreciate what really matters to you. Can you list down what would make you feel fulfilled and peaceful in your relationships? What would make you feel you are doing meaningful work? What would make you fulfilled as a parent?

A regular habit of Contemplation helps you find yourself. By understanding negative comparison and how it reduces your peace of mind, you can instead start focusing on your own strengths and living a more joyful and fulfilling life.

One of the most common dimensions where negative comparison occurs is academics. It's natural to look at classmates or friends who excel in their studies and feel like we're not measuring up. Maybe you compare your grades, test scores, or even the recognition and praise others receive.

Another dimension where negative comparison can arise is in our professional lives. We might compare our job titles, salaries, or career advancements to those of our colleagues or friends. You look at someone who was in college with you and think 'They've reached such heights. Where am I today?' This can lead to feelings of inadequacy and dissatisfaction with your own achievements.

Social comparison is quite prevalent around us today. Online platforms make it easy to compare yourself to others and their seemingly perfect lives. You might see carefully curated messages, filtered photos, and glamorous experiences, and feel like you're missing out or not living up to those standards.

You might compare your romantic relationship to those portrayed in movies, TV shows, your friends' relationships or what you might see other people portray online. This can lead to feelings of insecurity and dissatisfaction, and at times, disagreements with your partner.

Negative comparison often arises when it comes to physical appearance. You might see images of what society deems as the "ideal" body type or features and start to feel inadequate about your own appearance.

Negative comparison can have a profound impact on your peace of mind.

When you constantly compare yourself to others, it's easy to feel inadequate and question your own worth. You may begin to believe that you are not good enough or that your achievements pale in comparison to others'. This self-doubt and diminished self-worth can eat away your peace of mind and also prevent you from recognizing your unique talents, contributions, and strengths. Because you are so busy feeling bad about what you are not, you miss the crucial part of what you really are.

Negative comparison often triggers feelings of stress and anxiety. Constantly measuring yourself against others and worrying about how you stack up can lead to a constant state of unease. The pressure to meet certain standards or expectations can be overwhelming and affect your ability to find inner calmness and peace. In certain cases, people might resort to dangerous, irreversible actions in an attempt to find a solution to such stress.

Comparing yourself to others can also strain your relationships. When you are constantly focused on what others have and you don't, it might become difficult to enjoy what you do have with your loved ones. Moreover, this mindset may lead to jealousy or resentment toward the people you are comparing yourself to. This might disrupt your intimate conversations at home, creating distance and tension in your relationships with the ones you really care about because of the ones who may not really matter so much in your life.

When you are preoccupied with negative comparison, your energy is directed outward rather than inward. Instead of focusing on your own personal development and working on what makes you feel fulfilled, purposeful, and peaceful, you are consumed by what others are doing and how they are more or better than you. This mindset can prevent you from fully exploring your own potential and focusing on who you really are as a person.

This often leads to a perpetual state of dissatisfaction. When you are constantly comparing yourself to others, you may never feel satisfied with what you have achieved or where you are in life. This relentless pursuit of getting ahead of others rather than going deeper within yourself can leave you feeling empty and unfulfilled. To find your peace of mind, you must appreciate and focus on your own journey and find contentment in your own story, no matter how small, large, easy, difficult, plain or quirky it might be. It is yours, and that's what matters. Be true to your story. Make changes if necessary to make it more fulfilling, pleasant, joyful, peaceful, but know your story and own it.

If you don't ask what kind of family life will make me more peaceful, you might look for answers in the lives of those others who are merely focused on accumulating material possessions. Tyler and Kim asked this question and they decided that instead of owning one large, expensive house by the beach, they would rather purchase multiple smaller homes, in different cities, so they can travel as a family for long stays in their favorite places. Their fulfillment and peace come from experiencing the world together, without the stress of thinking about the costs or availability of hotels. Had they not asked that question, they might have fallen into the trap of keeping up with the Joneses.

To overcome negative comparison, you need to focus on your own values, strengths and ask yourself - What makes me feel more fulfilled, purposeful and peaceful? What's my story? - rather than focusing on what others are doing in their life. Through Contemplation, you need to find inner clarity and focus on living your own story rather than trying to live someone else's.

But why does negative comparison make you feel inferior?

Negative comparison generally makes you feel inferior not because you are actually inferior, but mostly because you are unclear. You haven't looked within to understand yourself well. You haven't created a deep connection with yourself to understand your values, strengths, motivations and what makes you more peaceful. What kind of partner would make me more peaceful? What kind of work will I find meaningful? What activities might increase my peace of mind and which ones might reduce it? Ask yourself these questions and you will quickly see that it is usually not your inferiority but your lack of internal clarity that is the real culprit.

To achieve internal clarity, you need to use your practice of Contemplation to delve into the depths of your being and truly understand who you are. It's about discovering your values, the things that matter most to you that also make you feel more at peace, and the passions that ignite a fire within you. Take the time to reflect on your strengths, those unique qualities that make you who you are. By recognizing these strengths, you can live a true version of who you really are. Sure, you will still need to work hard to improve in certain areas. But you will feel a certain contentment within you as you do that, because now you are looking within. You won't feel the sting of hollowness that you feel when you are constantly looking outside.

Self-discovery is a personal expedition, a path that only you can tread. It requires you to be open and honest with yourself, peering deep into your thoughts, emotions, and aspirations. Through Contemplation, you can gain insights into your motivations and desires. What truly drives you? What brings you joy, fulfillment and inner peace? What reduces your peace of mind? Am I living my own story or am I performing for the world?

Listen to the multiple voices inside your head as you explore your inner world and ask - What will make me peaceful? Not happy. Not wealthy. Not famous. Not smart. Not successful. Peaceful.

Writing can be a powerful tool in this process. By putting pen to paper, you can capture your thoughts and emotions, untangling the complexities of your mind. It allows you to express yourself freely, without judgment, and gain clarity along the way. When you use the Adios principle of right means peaceful, you can understand your mind a lot better and choose your actions wisely.

Contemplation also helps you still your mind and focus on one particular matter that is important to you. It is in these moments of stillness that you can connect with your inner wisdom, listen to various voices inside your mind and choose the right voice, the one that increases your peace of mind.

Seeking guidance from books or people experienced in self-discovery or coaches can also be valuable. They can offer fresh perspectives, ask thought-provoking questions, and help you navigate the twists and turns of your own journey. They can assist you in uncovering your true desires and aspirations, help you observe your biases and understand the path that aligns better with your phase of life and peace of mind. But you should be able to gather all that information and process it yourself during your Contemplation session so you can yourself get to the answer that is right for you, without depending on others too much. The answer needs to be right for you. That is what matters.

The journey of self-discovery is ongoing. As you go through various phases in your life, you may discover a new you along the way, sometimes more than once. Your state of mind, vision and what makes you feel peaceful may be different when you are looking for your first job, raising a child, leading an important mission, or looking forward to having grandchildren. You must constantly be in touch with your inner voices and have the ability to choose the voice that resonates with your well-being and inner peace, at every stage of your life. What stage of life are you at today?

By using Contemplation, you can acquire a deep understanding of yourself and live a life filled with purpose, authenticity, and peace of mind. Just get to know yourself really well. Be your best friend. Don't get lost in the external maze or how the world wants you to be. Be you. Be the you that is peaceful, not the you that is stressed and restless.

Each of us has something valuable, something that sets us apart. You have something that makes you you and I have something that makes me me. Out of so many other things that I could have done, I was driven toward Contemplation. I was also driven toward playing the drums. Not the guitar or the violin. That makes me me. What makes you you?

Ask yourself - what kind of work or relationship will make me feel more fulfilled and peaceful? The answer might be different for you and people close to you. That's your uniqueness. You feel strongly about something that many others may not, which means that a particular direction or action speaks to you much more than it speaks to others, and you feel something strongly about it. You need to be able to identify it. Put a finger on it.

That's your story. Your unique story. You need to live your story. Why? Because living your own story well will make you feel fulfilled and peaceful.

When it comes to learning, you might have a different learning style than your friends. You need to understand and appreciate that. Maybe slow and steady works better for you because you get to ponder on things more. Focus on your own learning journey and how it contributes to your overall well-being. You don't need to read 52 books in a year if that doesn't appeal to you. Maybe you want to read one book 52 times. Maybe you don't want to read at all. Being well-read is good. Being well-thought is even better.

Your work preferences may be different than many others because your life's non-financial vision might be very specific to what you believe in. If you are going to be spending many hours working each day, your work must be such that it aligns with your inner peace and gives you meaning or purpose. If it only offers you a paycheck in return for your soul, is that a transaction you are willing to undertake for many years? Find what work aligns with you and makes you more peaceful. It may not always be the one that is trending and popular. Sit alone, tune in and listen carefully. Do what resonates with you. Don't compare.

Your social preferences may be different from others. Imitating others may be tempting but may also bring restlessness along with it. The external world can be a meticulously curated display, not an accurate representation of reality. Your goal is to focus on knowing yourself and your own unique journey better so you can find fulfillment, purpose and inner peace. Your relationship may not be picture-perfect, but if it has depth - love, respect, care and friendship - that might be more fulfilling and meaningful than the many illusions you might witness outside.

Someone laughing loudly or looking confident or smiling ear to ear might not be really happy or peaceful on the inside. People can put on masks. Learn to look beyond them. Learn to look within. That's the best place to look for guidance.

Everyone's journey is different. Comparing yourself to others negatively is a fruitless exercise that can reduce your self-esteem and your peace of mind. Instead, turn your attention inward and appreciate the qualities that make you who you are. Find your own story and live that story well. By recognizing, appreciating, and living your own story, you can experience a sense of long-term fulfillment, purpose, and inner peace.

It is not usually inferiority but lack of internal clarity that causes negative comparison. Use Contemplation to be deeply connected with yourself, so you know yourself well. Where sharp internal clarity exists, negative comparison has no role to play.

CHAPTER TAKEAWAYS:

- Negative comparison usually exists not because you are really inferior to someone, but because you are unclear within.
- It can lead to a constant feeling of discontent and unhappiness. It can pervade various areas of your life,

such as academics, profession, social, intimate relationships, and physical appearance.

- The issue with negative comparison is that it concentrates on what you are missing rather than who you really are. It ignores your true self, your unique strengths and what energizes you.
- It ignores what will make you feel more fulfilled and peaceful and rather focuses on what other people might value or admire.
- Focus on your own story rather than trying to live someone else's.

∼

11. PRINCIPLE SEVEN: FEELS GOOD VS FEELS PEACEFUL

We all face dilemmas in life, one time or another, and sometimes really difficult ones.

We all need a system, a method to think through these difficult questions to find the answer that is right for us, the answer that will keep us peaceful. That's what matters in the end.

You're faced with a choice that could either make you feel good in the moment but bring stress in the long term or you sacrifice something today but that will bring you lasting peace of mind. Which option would you choose? Often, we find ourselves drawn toward immediate gratification without considering the long-term consequences on our overall well-being.

We learned earlier that whatever makes you more peaceful is right for you, and whatever makes you more restless or less peaceful is wrong for you. Now you need to take that a step forward and apply it to a situation that might feel good in the moment but might take away your peace of mind in the long run. This could be choosing between arguing with your partner / child or remaining silent, ingesting a harmful food item, or avoiding it, doing something immoral or staying on the right path, gossip about a colleague or let it pass, brag about something or be humble, or multiple other small and large decisions you might make during the day.

You have the power to choose between what feels good right now and what truly aligns with your inner peace. But it starts by directing your attention to your inner world, to how you feel within rather than how you appear to the world. You need to recognize the impact of your choices on your overall well-being.

You may be tempted to prioritize feeling good over feeling peaceful in various situations. It could be indulging in unhealthy habits, procrastinating on important tasks, or seeking validation from external sources. While these actions may provide temporary pleasure, they often disrupt your inner sense of calmness and create a less peaceful state of mind in the long run. By understanding the difference between feeling good and feeling peaceful, you can make conscious choices that align with your long-term well-being. It's about finding a balance between instant gratification and lasting contentment.

Your goal is not the pursuit of happiness. It is the pursuit of peace of mind. I don't mean you shouldn't be happy. Yes, happiness is good and desirable in life. But at the same time, you should also be able to clearly differentiate between what makes you happy only in the moment and what might increase your peace of mind in the long term. If an action gives you both, it is a great combination to have. If, however, it satisfies you only for a short while but is harmful for you in the long run, do you still want to do it?

We live in a world that constantly tempts us with quick fixes, immediate pleasures, and short-term gains. It's easy to get caught up in the desire for instant gratification without considering the long-term consequences.

You have likely experienced moments where you chose instant pleasure over what truly brings you peace. It could be indulging in unhealthy food when you know it's not good for your well-being, giving in to impulsive purchases that provide momentary excitement but leave you feeling regretful, seeking superficial validation from others to boost your self-esteem temporarily, or even choosing to be in a relationship just because it feels good in the moment or it fills a temporary void in your life without considering if that person is really the one for you.

While these choices may provide temporary pleasure, the question is, do you make them at the expense of your long-term peace of mind? It's important to recognize the patterns and triggers that lead you toward instant gratification. By practicing Contemplation to understand and observe your tendencies and motivations, you can begin to make such choices that enhance your inner peace and discard the ones that reduce it. It is about remaining aware of what you are doing and how it impacts your long term inner peace. When you think about it often, you remember. Hence Contemplation.

Think about an incident in the past when you opted for instant satisfaction and how it affected your overall well-being. Did it bring you lasting happiness and contentment, or did it leave you feeling empty and dissatisfied?

Temptations will always exist around you. Understanding your desires well, considering their long-term consequences and being clear about the kind of life you would like to live can help you manage life's temptations better and enable you to make choices that bring you lasting peace. Blaming a technology or a processed food company or the government isn't the solution. Your life is yours. Your peace of mind is your responsibility, no one else's. Not mine. Not your best friend's. Not your boss's. Yours. Contemplation on these principles will help you take charge of your life so you don't live on an autopilot mode and let the external world treat you like its puppet.

Sometimes, to create lasting peace, you need patience and delayed gratification. It means resisting the attraction of immediate pleasures and focusing on what makes you feel more fulfilled, purposeful and peaceful in the long run. True fulfillment comes from making choices that align with your values and contribute to your long-term well-being. Don't believe me. Try it and experience it for yourself.

When your primary focus is on pursuing short-term happiness, it's easy to fall into the trap of constant pleasure-seeking. While these experiences may provide temporary satisfaction and make you feel good in the moment, they often come at a cost. The more you rely on external sources to feel good, the more you become disconnected from your true self and your inner peace. Instead of finding long-term contentment within, you become dependent on external validation, material possessions, or fleeting moments of pleasure.

This constant pursuit of temporary pleasures can leave you feeling restless and unsatisfied. You may find yourself constantly chasing the next exciting experience, yet never truly finding lasting fulfillment. Moreover, relying on external validation for your sense of self-worth can be a never-ending cycle of seeking approval from others. Your happiness becomes contingent on the opinions and judgments of those around you. This external validation, however, is unreliable and inconsistent, leaving you vulnerable to fluctuations in other people's perceptions.

By solely focusing on momentary pleasures, you miss out on the deeper sense of peace and contentment that comes from knowing who you are and what makes you feel fulfilled and peaceful. When you know yourself deeply, you don't depend on external elements to find joy all the time. Looking for short-term happiness constantly can prevent you from making choices that lead to long-term fulfillment and genuine peace of mind.

Rather than constantly seeking external sources of validation and fleeting pleasures, it's crucial to cultivate a deeper connection with yourself. This involves understanding your values, passions, and purpose in life, understanding what will make you feel fulfilled, purposeful, and peaceful. Why? Because focusing on these elements usually provides peace of mind that lasts for a long time while the pleasure from external sources usually lasts for a very short period of time. So, as you go through your day, keep an eye on whether your actions in your personal and professional life provide you with long-term fulfillment or are they merely a source of short-term excitement.

Consider a scenario where you are in a romantic relationship with someone who constantly encourages you to engage in risky behaviors or make impulsive decisions. While these actions may provide a thrill or excitement in the moment, they can compromise your sense of peace and stability. You might find yourself constantly worried about the consequences of your actions and the impact they have on your well-being and future.

Similarly, ignoring serious red flags in your partner's behavior for the sake of immediate happiness or avoiding loneliness may lead to regret, a loss of self-respect or even mental trauma over time. Pretending to agree with your partner most of the time even when you don't just to avoid conflict may momentarily maintain harmony, but it often reduces your peace of mind and emotional intimacy in the relationship, leaving you longing for genuine connection and ultimately, stressed.

Imagine you come across a tempting offer to purchase a luxury that you've been desiring for a long time, even though it exceeds your budget. You decide to buy it anyway, believing it will bring you instant happiness. And it does. However, as time goes on, you realize that the financial strain caused by this impulsive purchase affects your overall peace of mind. You might find yourself constantly stressed about money, struggling to meet your day-to-day financial obligations. You might be sacrificing long-term financial security and your everyday peace of mind for a pleasure that lasted only a few days.

Consider a situation where you have the opportunity to take on a job that offers a higher salary but requires you to work longer hours and sacrifice your time with your spouse and child. Initially, the allure of a bigger paycheck feels enticing, and you may believe that the temporary discomfort of longer hours is worth the financial gain. However, as time passes, you start experiencing burnout, fatigue, and a diminished sense of well-being. It might also start affecting your relationship with your family negatively. You might not have the time to take care of your loved ones when they need you the most, which might weigh on your mind constantly, reducing your peace of mind overall.

Life is fairly hard to decipher so sometimes you learn by making mistakes. If you have made such a mistake with your work and family already and are now suffering because of that, make the right decision now. You do not have to continue to suffer for the next many years. Do what will make you peaceful in the long run. Do it now. Now is good. Now will work. It is never too late.

Similarly, engaging in office politics or undermining colleagues for personal gain may provide temporary satisfaction, but it often makes you more restless and hence less peaceful. This could also strain workplace relationships and affect your long-term personal growth, but the biggest disadvantage is internal - losing your own peace of mind.

Imagine you have been following a healthy lifestyle routine that includes regular exercise and a healthy diet. However, a friend invites you to consume excessive junk food or skip workouts, or even worse, indulge in harmful solid or liquid substances, all under the seductive guise of "treat yourself / you only live once / you deserve to live a good life." While it may feel good in the moment, over time, you may experience negative consequences on your physical and mental well-being. Your energy levels may decline, you may feel guilty or dissatisfied with your choices, your health may be compromised, and your overall peace of mind can be diminished.

There are moments when you as a parent may feel conflicted about your choices. For instance, you may indulge your child's every wish and desire, thinking it will make them happy. In the moment, it feels good to see their immediate joy, but deep down, you may question if you're instilling the right values in them. Handing them a piece of technology just to keep them busy so you can be free to do something seemingly important might feel like a relief at the moment, but you might be crippling them for the long term and setting them up for a life full of insecurity and stress. All this while genuinely believing that you always act in their best interest because you are a parent. True fulfillment as a parent might come from enabling your children to indepen-dently make such choices for themselves that will make them feel fulfilled, purposeful, and peaceful.

Imagine you are invited to a party where you know there will be excessive drinking and drug use. Although you are aware that engaging in such activities can have negative consequences on your health and overall well-being, you decide to join in to fit in with your peers and feel more "accepted" in the group. You choose feeling good in the moment over feeling peaceful in the long run. This could have long lasting harmful effects in your life. It can also lead to feelings of guilt, dependency, and a lack of inner peace.

Let's say you are seeking inner peace and meaning in your life. On this journey, you encounter a group or belief system that offers immediate answers and promises of enlightenment without requiring deep introspection or self-reflection. It may also offer interesting community events where you get to meet more like-minded people. You might also engage in intellectual discussions about the topics. Although it may feel exciting to adopt these beliefs at the moment, you may realize over time that they lack substance and do not align with your true inner values and purpose.

Meeting more people or going to a lot of community events may entertain you, enable you to make more friends and also help you release some emotional pain temporarily, but it may not necessarily lead to self-discovery. Intellectual discussions might make you feel more knowledgeable but may do nothing to improve your own practice. Emotional vulnerability of others might make you emotional in the moment and may help you connect with them better. But that's helpful in the external world, not in the internal world. It may not help you connect better with yourself. Choosing temporary pleasure, entertainment and socialization over a genuine spiritual journey can affect your journey toward self-knowledge and prevent you from finding lasting peace and fulfillment.

The rules that apply for making friends in the external world need to change if you are trying to make friends with yourself. If you continue to use your old habits of the external world and apply them to your progress in the internal world, you may not be able to go very far. You may experience some benefits, but to go deeper, you need to go inwards, not outwards.

So be clear about what you are doing and why. If you are only focused on making new friends, that's fine. But then don't expect to make much progress on your inner journey. Just know that you have chosen to socialize with others instead of socializing with yourself. The results will differ in both these cases. You could use such an environment as a starting point because everyone starts in their own manner and if you got started by joining such a group, it's useful because at least you got started. But if you wish to go deeper into your practice, you will need to move away from external discussion and focus more on your internal discussion. You may have started playing football on the street with a few friends, but to go from amateur to pro, you need to train differently. The same rule applies here.

This principle of feeling good vs feeling peaceful applies to multiple other situations in your life - the music you listen to, the clothes you choose to wear, the kind of physical exercise you choose to do, the kind of holidays you choose to go on, the location you choose to stay in, the kind of friends you choose to make, etc. In all these situations, there might be an option that feels good in the moment but is not really good for your long-term peace of mind. You might meet people who want to provoke your anger in the name of a social cause. That anger might feel good in the moment but ask yourself - Will this leave me peaceful in the long run?

Can you think of any such situations in your life right now?

You need to decide what is better for your peace of mind. Contemplation will help you do that.

In life, you often encounter situations where choosing to do something that feels bad in the moment can actually lead to long-term peace eventually. Discomfort, challenges, and difficult choices can also sometimes contribute to your overall well-being. Something that might feel bad in the short term might be right in the long term.

Imagine you are presented with an opportunity to pursue higher education or advance your career. The path requires intense dedication, long hours of studying, and sacrificing leisure time. Initially, this may make you feel bad as you experience stress, exhaustion, and a temporary lack of comfort. However, by persevering through the challenging journey, you acquire the necessary knowledge and skills that open doors to new opportunities and a sense of fulfillment. The temporary discomfort today leads to long-term personal growth in the future and a greater sense of peace in knowing that you have invested in yourself.

Consider the scenario where you decide to adopt a healthier lifestyle by incorporating regular exercise and a healthy diet. Initially, you may experience some physical discomfort or cravings for unhealthy foods. These temporary feelings of deprivation or discomfort might make you feel bad at the moment. However, by persisting and prioritizing your long-term health, you gradually experience increased energy, improved well-being, and a stronger sense of self-confidence.

Imagine you are in a toxic relationship or friendship that regularly pulls you down and negatively affects your well-being. It may be difficult to end the relationship as it can initially make you feel bad due to potential conflict or loneliness. However, by making the perhaps difficult and uncomfortable decision to stay away, you remove negative elements from your life and also make room for healthier relationships in the future that might bring you more peace.

Consider a situation where you decide to make financial sacrifices to pay off debts or save for a secure future. This may involve cutting back on unnecessary expenses, making budget adjustments, and foregoing immediate pleasure such as lavish shopping, parties, or purchases. Initially, these choices may make you feel unhappy as you experience the discomfort of a tight monthly budget. However, over time, your disciplined approach might lead to financial stability, reduced stress, and a sense of long-term security.

Let's say as you are going through the Adios system, you start to work on a situation in your life that brings up uncomfortable things from the past. It might feel bad to face them and avoiding them might feel more comfortable in the moment. But if you go through the process, use the Adios principles and finally resolve those thorny issues once and for all, you will feel a lot lighter, content, and peaceful in the long run.

Imagine that at work you have a competent subordinate who consistently displays toxic behavior. They may excel in their tasks and deliver quality work, but their negative attitude, constant criticism, and disrespectful behavior constantly create an unhealthy atmosphere that stresses out other members in the team and also negatively affects your own well-being.

Initially, the thought of firing a competent colleague may make you feel bad due to an immediate loss of work efficiency. However, by making the difficult decision to let them go, you might be able to create a more positive and healthy work environment. People might be able to breathe better, hence work more productively. Choosing to prioritize the overall well-being of the team over short-term productivity or profits can lead to a better work environment in the long run. A happier, mentally fit team can perform significantly better compared to a team that is stressed due to a toxic environment at the workplace.

Moreover, by choosing to address the issue head on and take appropriate action, you demonstrate to your colleagues and superiors that you stand for and value a respectful and supportive work environment. While it may feel bad to let go of a competent colleague at the moment, the long-term benefits such as increased job satisfaction, improved mental well-being, and a more peaceful and productive work environment should soon outweigh the short-term cost.

If you are a business leader, you might face a situation where taking an investment from someone or going through with a huge business deal might be very tempting. But if you know that the investor or that deal isn't really aligned with your values and vision and will eventually reduce your peace of mind, it might be wiser to let it go and bite the bullet in the short term. It might sting you today, but if you wait a little longer, you will find something that is right for you. You just need to fight your impatience to make quick progress. Fast may sound exciting, but it is not always better. Moving forward quickly at any cost is less important than moving forward in the right direction.

Sometimes feeling bad for a few moments today can lead to feelings of fulfillment and inner peace for many more moments in the long run. So always ask yourself - Even though it feels bad in the moment, will this make me more peaceful in the long run? Is there a bigger picture here that I must see and respect?

When it comes to making choices in life, focus on your peace of mind and don't get carried away by momentary pleasure or satisfaction.

Master your inner voices, and in a critical situation, take a moment to pause and reflect on what feels right to you, what feels more peaceful to you. Tune in to your instincts and pay attention to the subtle signals within. Your inner voices guide you toward your actions, but you must have the ability to choose the right voice, the one that makes you more peaceful and let go of the voice that makes you more restless or less peaceful. Remember that the loudest voice inside your head is not necessarily the right voice. Your mind is not always your friend. Choose the voice that makes you more peaceful and fulfilled in the long run. If you make a wrong choice, you will learn soon. Try again next time. With practice, you will get much better at it.

In complex or difficult situations, clarity may be hard to come by. It's natural to feel uncertain or overwhelmed. During such times, take a step back and make time for Contemplation. Consider seeking advice from trusted mentors, friends, or professionals who can offer valuable insights, but remember to take that advice and use your own Contemplation to find your answer, the answer that is right for you, that makes you more peaceful in the long run. Ultimately, the goal is to gain such clarity that helps you to make choices that align with your peace of mind, and not the kind of clarity that makes you more excited or restless.

Say a definite "No" to a choice that does not align with your peace of mind. No. Period. Not Yes. Not Maybe. No. This allows you to set healthy boundaries, protect your well-being, and allow into your life only that which truly matters to your long-term inner peace. Do not buckle under the pressure of friends, colleagues, competitors, or the stock market to do things that are not healthy for you. Listen to the voice that makes you feel more peaceful in the long run. That's your true friend. Contemplation will help you find the courage to follow that voice without feeling any external pressure. You define what is acceptable for your well-being and only let those things into your life.

Maybe you made a few mistakes in your life. Maybe you made a few bad choices in your life. Or maybe you made many bad choices in your life, and you wake up every day and it is so hard. You wish that you could go back in time and live your life over again without all those bad choices you made. But you can't, and none of that matters anymore. What matters is that you are here today, reading this, thinking about it and willing to make new choices starting today. That's what matters.

If you change your input today, the output tomorrow will change. If you change the way you think and act starting today, your tomorrow will change. It seems difficult because you look at your future through your lens of the past. Discard that lens. Get a new lens from today. The Adios lens. Make new choices from today, right this moment, and tomorrow will start to become nothing like yesterday.

By consciously making choices aligned with your peace of mind, you take control of your life's direction, rather than letting a restless mind influenced by the restless external world take charge of your life. When you make your decisions with the knowledge of right and wrong - what makes you more vs less peaceful - you can make life's choices thoughtfully and clearly which will help you create a life of peace, meaning and fulfillment.

In which dimensions of your life today can you apply the ADIOS principle of Feels Good vs Feels Peaceful?

_____

_____

_____

MARK'S ADIOSCOPE

Situation

As a married man, my business trips spark an inner conflict. Part of me feels tempted to indulge in extramarital affairs, craving that excitement. I engage in flirty behavior that pulls me toward giving in. Sometimes I do cross the line. But then guilt sets in, weighing on me. I feel torn between temporary gratification versus honoring my commitment to my wife.

Twin Voices:

The first voice is that of temptation and desire. It seduces me with excitement and temporary pleasure. This voice likes flirtatious conversations and the thrill of extramarital affairs. But the second voice is that of shame. The voice reminds me of my commitment and the promises I made to my wife. This voice carries the heavy burden of guilt, recognizing that my actions are not right. It is the part of me that understands the consequences of giving in to temptation and seeks alignment with what feels right in my heart.

Following Voice 2 will make me more peaceful.

Right vs Wrong (more vs less peaceful)

Whenever I am out on a business trip, I feel a pang of restless-ness. The thrill of the chase, new encounters, clinking glasses – it stirs something in me, something inside me that is always looking for the next high. But when that high subsides, all that's left is a mountain of guilt, a hollow emptiness that no amount of fleeting pleasure can fill. I feel terrible about the kind of husband I am.

I want peace that isn't punctured by guilt or regret, peace that lasts for a long time, unlike the pleasure that lasts only for a short while. And I believe the path to that peace isn't through a series of fleeting encounters but through the lasting bond I share with my wife.

Anything that increases my peace of mind is right for me. I need to stop chasing the thrill and focus on what truly matters – my relationship with my wife, my commitment to her, and our shared dreams and goals. And if my daughter were to ever find out about this, I would lose my respect in her eyes forever.

Negative Comparison:

I have also been influenced by a colleague at work who is called the Casanova of the office. He regularly indulges in such flings and is always in the limelight for his adventures. His behavior made me ask myself - Am I not smart enough to get all those girls if he can? In that moment of false pride, I forgot about my true love and commitment toward my wife and kids and started trying to score higher than him in a game I'm not so proud of playing. Very naive of me. I need to be more connected with myself and what makes me more peaceful in the long run.

Feels good vs feels peaceful:

Hooking up with someone new, the excitement of flirtation and temporary escapes from my marital responsibilities, feel good. I indulge in those fleeting pleasures without considering the impact on my commitment to my wife and the guilt that would follow.

However, deep down, I know that my choices don't make me feel right in my heart. I carry a heavy burden of guilt; torn between the temporary pleasure and the commitment I have made to my wife. What feels good in the moment does not bring me lasting peace of mind.

AMELIA'S ADIOSCOPE

Situation

I'm conflicted about having a baby. My friend says I'll figure it out, but doubts linger. I worry about giving up my dreams and independence. Watching happy families stirs up envy and fear. I'm unsure if I'm cut out for motherhood. Talking to my mom helped a bit. She says it's challenges and joy, follow my heart. But I still don't know what decision is right. This responsibility scares me, yet part of me wants it.

Twin Voices:

One voice is that of fear, cautioning me about the immense responsibility and unknown challenges that come with being a mother. It reminds me of the sleepless nights, the sacrifices of personal freedom I would need to make (Friday night outs, girl movie nights, quarterly vacations) and the potential impact on my career.

Voice 2 is the one rooted in a deep longing for motherhood. It reminds me of the joys and fulfillment that come with raising a child. This voice encourages me to accept the transformative experience of becoming a parent with open arms.

There is a voice of the society that tells me that it's the "right" time to have a baby, so you better do it now.

I think there is a fourth voice as well, logically analyzing the situation. It asks me - do you have enough money to raise a baby, are you really ready to be a mother you silly girl, what will happen to your marriage once you have a child? Sounds similar to Voice 1.

Right vs Wrong (more vs less peaceful)

What would you write here?

Feels good vs feels peaceful:

ıld you write here?

DIOSCOPE

Never regret your
mistakes. Admire
the courage it
took to attempt
the unknown.

...ıle I am fairly successful as a business leader, I long for more constantly. I want to have a private jet, just like a few other famous leaders. This makes me behave recklessly sometimes, because I want to quickly show success to my Board without considering the long-term consequences of my actions. In some cases, I haven't paid much attention to consequences, and in a few others, I have deliberately turned a blind eye toward potential negative outcomes, because I want to deliver a short-term spike in my numbers.

Twin Voices

What would you write here?

Right vs Wrong (more vs less peaceful)

What would you write here?

Feels good vs feels peaceful:

What would you write here?

CHAPTER TAKEAWAYS:

- If doing or saying something feels good, also remember to ask - will it also make me feel peaceful in the long run?
- Sometimes, it might feel bad in the short run, but might be the right thing to do for the long run.
- Temptations will always remain around you. When you make your decisions, think about what will make you feel more fulfilled and peaceful in the long term.

12. THE POWER OF YOUR VOICE

You have a unique voice that can influence and inspire others if you choose to do so. Whether you realize it or not, your words have the ability to shape your world and the world around you.

You are a one-of-a-kind individual, and your voice is just as unique as you are. It carries the essence of who you are, revealing your thoughts, feelings, and experiences to the world. When you speak, you have the power to convey who you are and leave a lasting impact on others.

Close your eyes and listen to the sound of your own voice. Hear the rhythm, the tone, and the energy behind your words. Notice the emotions that emerge as you speak from your heart. This is your voice, a reflection of your innermost thoughts and feelings.

You need to appreciate the strength and potential that lies within your voice. It is a powerful tool that can inspire, motivate, and touch the lives of others. Just as a painter uses paint and brushes to create art or a musician plays different notes to compose a melody, your voice has its own unique way of leaving a mark on others.

Your voice is not just about the words you say, but also about the intention and authenticity behind them. When you speak with conviction and passion, your voice becomes a force. It becomes energy that has the ability to resonate with others and inspire them to get things done, move things forward. If you speak with a healthy intention, an honest intention, you can build connections that go beyond surface-level interactions. The listener can feel that authenticity.

While we are used to thinking about our voice primarily as a tool to speak to the external world, your voice also plays a big, very big role in determining your own peace of mind. A lot has been said about how to use your speech to make an impression on others, but that is an outside focused approach. You must pay immense attention to what your speech does to you on the inside - does it make you feel more peaceful, or does it increase your restlessness? What you say and how you say it, how much you speak, the velocity, tone, cadence, and volume of your speech play a significant role in whether you feel more peaceful or more restless on a daily basis, and eventually in life. So, while you focus on how you can use your voice in the outside world, do not forget to first assess its impact on your inside world.

Your voice is more than just words. It is a doorway to your inner world, a vessel through which you can express your thoughts, beliefs, and emotions. When you speak from your heart, you have the power to connect with others on a profound level.

Your voice allows you to share your ideas, perspectives, and experiences with those around you. Whether it's sharing your ideas in a classroom discussion, making a presentation to your Board of Directors or a customer, or delivering a heartfelt speech to a team or your nation, your voice carries the ability to leave a lasting impact.

When you speak honestly and passionately, your voice can become a source of inspiration. It has the power to ignite passion in others, motivating them to pursue their dreams and appreciate their own unique voices, or believe in a cause larger than themselves. It can give them the courage to do something they believe in but feel a little weak to move forward with.

However, it is also important to recognize the potential consequences of not using your voice in a healthy manner.

Using your voice to spread negativity, engage in hurtful gossip, or manipulate others into undertaking unhealthy actions, can also have long-term damaging effects. It can strain relationships and create a toxic environment. If taken to an extreme, it can harm people physically and mentally.

The power of your voice lies not only in what you say but also in how you say it. When you speak with kindness and respect, you create an atmosphere of warmth and well-being. Your words have the potential to uplift and inspire others. But the opposite is also true. You can use your voice wisely to build bridges of love, or you can use it to start a war. You can use it to help others, or to provoke a team of engineers to harm others.

Appreciate the capabilities of your voice, but also recognize the responsibility that comes with it. Use your voice in a way that creates a more fulfilling, purposeful and peaceful life for you and everyone else concerned.

Throughout history, the human voice has been used as a powerful instrument for both positive and negative purposes. In the personal, business, political, and other dimensions, some individuals have utilized their voices to inspire, bring about positive change, and promote peace, while others have used their voices to spread discord, incite violence, fuel conspiracy theories, spread false information and manipulate others to further their own selfish agendas.

Your voice is powerful and has the potential to have an immense impact on you personally as well as the external world. It holds the potential to either build bridges or burn them. It holds the potential to either create peace or destroy it. It holds the potential to either spread the truth or to suppress it.

Use your voice to create a fulfilling, purposeful and peaceful life for yourself and the ones around you. If you are in a position to influence many other people, you need to be even more careful about the quality of your influence. You doing something wrong is one thing. A hundred other people doing it because your wrongdoing influenced them can be dangerous. You don't want to be that person.

If you are a teacher, use your voice to inspire your students to choose a career that will enhance their long-term inner peace and maximize their potential.

If you are a product owner, use your voice to inspire your team to ship products that do not create restlessness and insecurity but enhance peace and fulfillment.

If you are a partner, use your voice to convey love, care and respect toward your partner, so they feel secure and warm.

If you are a parent, use your voice to create an environment at home that inspires your child to look inward and find answers that bring them fulfillment, purpose, and peace of mind.

If you are a leader, use your voice to motivate others to have the courage to choose the path that is peaceful rather than the path that seems exciting in the moment.

Your voice is a very powerful tool. Use it wisely.

If you are a leader, pause for a minute, look away and ask yourself this question right now - Am I in a position to influence the thoughts and actions of others? Do some people look up to me? If the answer is Yes, take a minute to formally acknowledge it to yourself - So I have the power to influence others. How should I use this power? Use it strategically to influence others in a manner that will make them more peaceful or use it to mislead them for attaining my selfish personal goals?

Also, while you use your voice to speak to others, you also use your internal voice to speak to yourself. Spend time with yourself to understand the various voices inside of you, and choose the one that brings you lasting fulfillment, meaning and peace of mind, rather than the one that constantly puts you down or increases your restlessness. When you increase the volume of the inner voice that inspires you to be positive, confident, and peaceful, the negative voice will gradually disappear.

Your voice is your special power. Use it strategically, but wisely.

CHAPTER TAKEAWAYS:

- Your voice has a very big impact on your own peace of mind. What you say, how you say it, how much you speak, the pace of your speech and the tone and volume of your speech practically determine whether you will live a peaceful or a restless life.
- Your voice can also have a significant impact on others around you. You can use it to inspire healthy behavior or to provoke negativity.
- If you are a leader, acknowledge that you are in a position to influence others around you. Use the power of your voice strategically, but wisely, in a manner that enables people to become more fulfilled and peaceful, rather than become stressful and restless.

∼

13. PRINCIPLE EIGHT: QUALITY OF SPEECH

Your words have a powerful effect on how you feel inside. The things you say not only affect others but also determine your own peace of mind. If you tend to use negative speech in your interactions at home, work or outside, it will reduce your inner peace.

Negative speech means speech that tends to reduce your peace of mind, like criticism, sarcasm, anger, gossip, and complaining. When you engage in negative speech, it creates a toxic environment within your mind. It's like a cycle of negativity that keeps going round and round, making you feel restless and unhappy.

When you criticize or say hurtful things, it reinforces negative thoughts and emotions within yourself. Even after you've spoken those negative words, they continue to play on your mind, making you think more negative thoughts. It might feel good for a moment to criticize someone or complain about something, but it actually reduces your peace of mind for a very long time. Please note that we are talking about the impact of negative speech on your own peace of mind, not how it affects someone else.

Constantly repeating negative speech, say at home or with friends or colleagues, can cause mental and emotional distress. Do you tend to do this today? Does that increase your inner peace or reduce it? By being aware of the quality of your speech, you can understand how your words affect your state of mind.

Reducing negative speech doesn't mean hiding your emotions or avoiding difficult conversations. It means finding healthier ways to express yourself. You can still be assertive and honest but without resorting to negative or hurtful language. It might take some practice, but it's easier than you think.

Because of the sheer amount of talking, you might do during the day, every single day, your speech might practically determine whether you will live a peaceful or a restless life. By reducing negative speech, you can create a calmer and more peaceful mind. Instantly. Try it for a week and see how it feels.

Negative speech can become a never-ending cycle if you are not careful about it. It can start with one negative word or comment, and before you know it, it keeps going on and on.

When you engage in negative speech, it feeds into negative thoughts and emotions within yourself. For example, if you criticize someone, it might temporarily make you feel better or superior. But deep down, it strengthens negative patterns in your mind, making it easier for you to criticize again in the future. You have done it once, so it is familiar now, and it also felt good for a bit. You want to do it again. And again.

The more you engage in negative speech, the more it becomes a habit. It's like a loop that keeps repeating itself. You might find yourself constantly complaining, gossiping, or getting angry. This cycle of negative speech can be exhausting and draining, both for you and the people around you.

Negative speech not only affects your own peace of mind but also impacts your relationships with others. When you constantly criticize or speak negatively, it creates a tense and toxic atmosphere. People may start avoiding you or feel uncomfortable in your presence, and sometimes you may never come to know that is the case because people usually hesitate to tell you such a thing directly. Avoiding you is easier.

If you have ever known a very negative person who was close to you, think about how you felt the moment they walked into the room. What did you think? How did you feel? Did you want them to stay, or did you hope that they would leave as quickly as possible? Did you avoid going near them sometimes? If you become that person, others will feel the way you felt and might avoid you, and they may never tell you what they are thinking.

To eliminate your negative speech, start by paying attention to the words and the tone you use when you speak to your partner, colleagues, friends, parents, children, someone at a coffee shop or a supermarket, etc. and the impact they have on you. How do you feel when you speak? Does that leave you more peaceful or more restless? This awareness is very powerful. Catch yourself when you're about to engage in negative speech and pause for a moment. Ask yourself if it's really necessary or if there's a more positive way to express yourself, or if you can remain silent.

What's on your agenda for the next few days? Do you see yourself being around people where you might tend to use negative speech? Set a reminder for ten minutes prior to that event so you are aware of that tendency and prepare yourself to not speak negatively. This will help you be more thoughtful when you speak.

If you engage in some kind of negative speech with someone, ask yourself:

- Did that increase my peace of mind or decrease it?
- Could I avoid it next time?

Your words have the power to define your inner peace. By removing negative speech from your conversations, you will feel lighter and more peaceful.

The most damaging impact of negative speech is on your own peace of mind. If, for a minute, you ignore what such speech does to people around you or how it affects your relationships with others and only focus on what it does to you, you will realize that in most cases it leaves you less peaceful or more restless.

Your goal is the pursuit of peace of mind. If negative speech reduces your peace of mind, you must remove it from your life. Apart from harming your own peace of mind directly, your negative speech can affect various other aspects of your life, which in turn might reduce your overall peace of mind.

Imagine a situation where you frequently criticize or speak harshly to your family members, friends, or romantic partner. This may be because of frustration, anger, or a desire to assert control over them. However, this negative speech leaves a lasting impact on those around you. It makes them feel disrespected, unappreciated, and emotionally hurt.

When you engage in negative speech, you send a message that you are not accepting others for who they are. Instead of supporting and uplifting them, you tear them down with your words. You find faults in them. You put them down. This creates a toxic atmosphere and leads to emotional distance and strained relationships.

When you speak harshly, your words are often fueled by emotions or the urge to prove someone wrong rather than a genuine desire to find resolution. This can lead to you living in a constant state of restlessness and stress.

By using negative speech, you might win an argument or two, but you might lose the relationship. Something that gives you a high in the short term is not necessarily good for you in the long term. What feels good is not necessarily right for you. Choose your words carefully.

Internal negative speech also matters a lot. The way you speak to yourself internally affects your self-esteem and overall confidence. When you engage in negative self-talk or constantly put yourself down, it undermines your self-worth and hampers your ability to reach your full potential.

Life is full of challenges. Let's say you make a mistake or face a setback. Instead of acknowledging it as a learning experience or a temporary setback, you indulge in negative self-speech. You may say things like, "I'm so stupid," or "I'm no good at anything." This internal negative dialogue reduces your self-esteem and weakens your belief in your own abilities.

When you consistently engage in self-deprecating talk, you might begin to view yourself through a distorted lens. You might fail to recognize your strengths, talents, and accomplishments, focusing solely on perceived shortcomings or failures. This constant self-criticism creates a negative self-image and erodes your confidence, making it difficult to take on new challenges or risks.

Moreover, negative self-speech limits your potential by instilling a fear of failure and a lack of belief in your abilities. It becomes a self-fulfilling prophecy, where you subconsciously undermine your own success by doubting yourself and holding yourself back. The more you engage in negative self-speech, the more it becomes a habitual pattern that reinforces low self-esteem and self-doubt.

The words you speak also deeply affect your emotional well-being. When negative speech becomes a regular part of your communication, it reinforces negative emotions within yourself, leading to a constant state of anger, frustration, or sadness.

Think about a time when you engaged in negative speech or complained incessantly. How did it make you feel? Chances are, it didn't uplift your spirits or bring you joy. Instead, it likely intensified negative emotions and left you feeling drained, dissatisfied and less peaceful.

Negative speech acts as a constant reminder of the things that bother you or the aspects of your life that you perceive as negative. By continuously expressing negativity, you reinforce those negative emotions within yourself, causing them to become deeply ingrained in your mindset.

Let's say you constantly complain about your job or a colleague. Each time you engage in negative speech about it, you remind yourself of the aspects you dislike, the frustrations you face, and the unhappiness you experience. And by speaking in that manner, you experience a temporary feeling of release, a sort of pleasant satisfaction in the short term. But this repetitive negative talk slowly intensifies your negative emotions, leaving you less peaceful and more restless at the end of the day.

Think about it: when you constantly complain about your tasks, deadlines, or colleagues, what are you really doing? What are you spending your time on? How are you spending your energy? You are spending your time and energy on the negative aspects of the situation rather than seeking solutions or finding ways to improve. Whatever you spend your time and energy on grows and develops further. The question is - what do you wish to develop?

Your words have a significant impact on how others perceive you in social settings. When you engage in negative speech, such as gossiping or speaking ill of others, it can have detrimental effects on your social relationships.

Gossiping or speaking negatively about others creates a negative reputation for yourself. People around you may start to see you as someone who spreads negativity and cannot be trusted with personal information.

When people observe you engaging in negative speech frequently, they may become cautious about sharing their thoughts, feelings, or personal experiences with you. They may fear that you will speak negatively about them as well, since it is your habit to do so.

It is our natural tendency to hold onto things we love and avoid things we don't. But this also applies to unpleasant things. If you use negative speech frequently and repeatedly (say repeatedly criticizing an event or a person), you need to understand that at some level internally, you actually love doing it because it provides you with some kind of satisfaction. You have developed a certain liking for negative speech, even though it might sound politically incorrect. You might resist by saying "Why would I ever do that? Who wants to be angry all the time?" but if you examine it quietly, silently, on your own, you might see what is really going on in your mind. Don't focus on proving something to others. Look within, quietly, and understand what is really going on. Do it for yourself.

This is the reason why you must take your Contemplation journey alone, so you can understand yourself better quietly and make the necessary changes that will ultimately leave you more peaceful. Working alone enables you to avoid embarrassment before others or their unnecessary judgment and instead get straight to the root of the problem and solve it. Not merely soothe the symptoms temporarily but solve the root of the problem. Don't make it more difficult for yourself. Adios stands for A Dialogue In Objective Silence. Have that dialogue with yourself, objectively, without any bias, alone in silence.

Negative speech can occur due to many reasons. In moments of frustration, negative speech can become a way to vent your emotions and let off steam. When you encounter challenges or setbacks, it's natural to feel overwhelmed and seek an outlet to express your frustrations. Negative speech may seem like a quick solution to release pent-up emotions and find temporary relief.

Expressing your frustrations by using rude words or profanity might provide a sense of temporary release. It might allow you to vent your anger, disappointment, or dissatisfaction with a situation or person. However, regularly using negative expressions will consistently reduce your peace of mind. Take a moment and ask yourself how you feel - more peaceful or more restless? Satisfied, perhaps. But peaceful? So whenever you say 'F... it', remember that 'it' actually refers to your own peace of mind. You are effing your peace of mind.

Continuously engaging in negative speech means your mind remembers the negative aspects of that situation a lot more, so you find it harder to see the positive aspects. What is repeated is remembered. This can trap you in a state of constant discontent and severely impact your peace of mind and overall well-being.

Most peace-loving people don't want to be around those who are negative all the time, so if you use negative speech frequently, you might be left with only negative people around you. That is not a good environment to be in. Yes, they might be friends, but ask yourself - does this environment encourage me to become more peaceful or is it making me a more negative person and decreasing my peace of mind? This could be at work, at the gym, or even old friends. Think about it.

To break free from the cycle of frustration and negative speech, it's crucial to find healthier outlets for your emotions. Contemplation on the Adios principles helps you become acutely aware of what is making you less peaceful. When you realize that frequent negative speech is taking away your peace of mind, this awareness helps you reduce it. By focusing on your Vision Planner, you also begin to focus on things that matter to you and maximize your potential and peace of mind, rather than spending your time and energy on elements in your life that are draining your energy.

Sometimes, negative speech arises from your own fears and insecurities. When you feel threatened or unsure about yourself, you may resort to criticizing, being angry or sarcastic, or passing judgment on others. It becomes a defense mechanism—a way for you to protect yourself and feel temporarily superior or in control.

For example, imagine you are a business leader and you're feeling insecure about your own leadership abilities. Instead of working on improving your own abilities, you might engage in negative speech by making fun of other leaders who might be more successful than you are. By putting them down, you momentarily feel a false sense of superiority. However, this negative speech does nothing to help you improve so you can overcome your fear or insecurity. The fundamental problem remains.

Let's say you're starting a new job, and you're feeling anxious about fitting in. In an attempt to feel more accepted, you might engage in negative speech by gossiping about your colleagues or finding faults in their work. While this might provide a temporary sense of support from a few people who also indulge in such behavior, it will damage the trust and camaraderie within the workplace, ultimately affecting your own peace of mind and job satisfaction.

Overcoming negative speech rooted in fear and insecurity requires self-reflection and courage. It's important to recognize and address the underlying fears and insecurities that drive this behavior. Understand your mind. Don't waste your time feeling guilty about something. You might have lost your way over the past few months or years. Understand the problem and do something to fix it.

Contemplation on the Adios principles helps you see things more clearly, which helps you choose those actions that make you more peaceful and shun the ones that make you more restless or less peaceful. For example, using the principle of Looking Inward vs Outward, you might realize that focusing too much on fitting in or pleasing others does not really serve you well and you should spend your energies in pursuits that bring you fulfillment and inner peace, the ones that you might have listed in your Vision Planner.

Sometimes, you might use negative speech because it's something you learned from your surroundings. If you grew up in an environment where rude or bad words were common, like people constantly criticizing or gossiping or using profanity, you might start doing the same without even realizing it. These behaviors become a part of your speech patterns very naturally. But with effort, you can unlearn them and wherever necessary, replace them with positive speech.

Let's say you grew up with friends who often spoke negatively about others. They would criticize and say unpleasant things about people behind their backs. As you spent time with them, you started picking up these negative speech habits, including certain words that you might otherwise not have used. Now, even when you don't want to, you sometimes find yourself saying mean things about others using unpleasant words without realizing the impact it has on your own peace of mind.

This could also happen if you start watching too many movies that use negative language. It settles into your subconscious mind.

Just because you learned negative speech doesn't mean you have to continue using it. You can willingly choose a different way of speaking whenever you want. By becoming aware of these learned behaviors and their negative effects, with a little bit of practice, you can change yourself completely.

One way to unlearn negative speech is by being mindful of your words. You can use the Adios principle of reducing your quantity of speech / adding silence in such a situation. During your daily Contemplation practice, review the events that occurred during the day and analyze where you used negative speech during that day. Becoming aware is a very powerful change in your personality. Next, begin to work on that behavior starting the next day.

Before speaking, pause and think about whether what you're about to say is negative or hurtful. Ask yourself if it contributes positively to the conversation or if it will create negativity. By being conscious of your speech, you can make a deliberate effort to either stay silent or choose kinder and more positive words in the conversation.

Another helpful approach is surrounding yourself with people who do not use negative speech. Seek out people who use positive speech and engage in uplifting conversations, or at the very least, don't use negative speech in their conversations. Avoid environments that use negative speech frequently. In some cases, this might mean changing your social circle, the movies you watch, the gym you go to or the company you work for. Some decisions might be harder than others, but it depends on how serious you are about your peace of mind. Just like you adopted negative speech from your old environment, you can learn to eliminate it from your vocabulary by spending time in your new, non-negative / positive environment.

Sometimes, you might use negative speech because you want validation or attention from others. When you say negative things, especially about other people, it can grab people's attention and make them react to what you're saying. This can make you feel important or validated, even if it's only for a short time. But relying on negative speech for validation keeps you stuck in a cycle of negativity and reduces your inner peace. Relationships based on anger or hatred can seem very strong, but they are bad for your peace of mind.

Let's say you are a banker working in a competitive financial institution. You observe that some of your colleagues receive attention when they engage in gossip or speak negatively about their clients or colleagues, especially over alcohol. They might criticize their clients' financial decisions or spread unhealthy rumors about their more capable coworkers. Seeing this, you might be tempted to join in, believing that it will make you popular. However, this can take away your own inner peace and also damage your professional reputation with clients and colleagues. If you plan to remain in that industry for a long time, the word may go around and your negative reputation might precede you, something that might not be very easy to wash off in the future. This might lead to you not being able to maximize your potential and hence reduce your peace of mind in the long run.

For some individuals, negative speech becomes a habitual pattern that is difficult to break. If you have been engaging in negative speech for a long time, it can become ingrained in your communication style and automatic responses. Breaking free from these patterns requires conscious awareness and a commitment to avoiding negative speech and adopting more positive speech.

As an artist, you may have faced numerous rejections or critiques of your work. Over time, this can lead to a negative mindset and negative internal speech about your own abilities. You might constantly criticize your own artwork, belittle your talent, or compare yourself unfavorably to other artists. This habitual pattern of negative self-talk can affect your creative process and prevent you from fully expressing your artistic potential.

By using a regular habit of Contemplation, you become more aware of what makes you more peaceful and what makes you more restless. By using the principle of feeling good vs feeling peaceful, you might realize that this kind of negative self-talk might provide you instant satisfaction, but it is eroding your overall peace of mind and also harming your ability to become a better artist. This can help you set up systems - for example multiple reminders on your phone - that help you keep track of what you say or do during the day so you can take a moment to reflect on your speech and actions and choose only those that enhance your inner peace.

Negative speech is not good for your peace of mind. Whether used in the outside world or while talking to yourself, it will eventually only damage your inner peace. Be more aware of what you say and how you say it. You might speak a lot during the day. The higher the negativity in your speech, the lower your peace of mind.

CHAPTER TAKEAWAYS:

- Negative speech such as criticism, sarcasm, anger, gossip, and complaining reduce your peace of mind.
- Stay away from environments where people use negative speech frequently. Seek environments where negative speech is absent or where people speak in a healthy and respectful manner.
- Using negative speech can become addictive as the more you use it, the stronger your internal negative mental pattern becomes.
- You might use negative speech with your family, friends, at work or with strangers. Be careful about what you say and how you say it.
- Ask yourself - Is this negative speech making me more peaceful or is it taking away my peace of mind?

14. PRINCIPLE NINE: QUANTITY OF SPEECH

Silence is not just the absence of sound; it is a powerful tool that can bring you peace, clarity, and deep inner connection.

Silence provides an environment for reflection, introspection, and deep understanding. When you add silence to your speech, you are able to quiet your mind and tune in to your inner voice. Your inner voice might be trying to say something to you, but if you are too busy speaking, you may never hear it.

In the midst of noise and constant stimulation, silence allows you to find peace. It is in these moments of quiet that you can truly listen to yourself. And others. Silence gives you the chance to slow down, observe your thoughts and emotions, and find your answers within.

In addition to peace, silence also helps you find clarity. When you pause and allow yourself to be still and quiet, your Contemplation practice can help you gain a clearer perspective on your life and the challenges you face. It is in these moments that you can hear the voices in your head a lot more clearly and can effectively understand which voice will lead to a more fulfilling, purposeful and peaceful life.

Clarity also has its shades, or levels. It isn't always about whether you are clear about something or not. Yes or No. Sometimes, it is also about how clear you are. For instance, initially you might not have a certain perspective about a situation but with Contemplation you might get one. You feel a sense of clarity about it. But clarity isn't a 0 or 1 phenomenon. It is a spectrum. If you continue to think deeply about it, in many cases you might see your clarity getting better, sharper. You might see your conviction getting stronger. So just knowing 'I should do this' might be Level 1 clarity. Feeling 'I should do this' in every cell of your body is Level 10 clarity. Silence will help you get there.

However, finding silence in a busy and distracted world can be a challenge. We are constantly bombarded with noise from the demands of our daily lives. Our attention is pulled in multiple directions, making it difficult to carve out moments of silence.

Here is something I want you to embed in your mind. Write this down in your notes and put a thick box around it. If you wish to make any progress at all in your journey of self-knowledge, incorporating regular silence in your life is an absolute must. Without that, you will make no progress in the real sense. You might become a self-knowledge scholar, write papers on it, deliver keynotes on it, but you won't experience it. You won't embody it. You won't feel it deep within. Silence is not optional or nice-to-have on this path. It is an absolute must.

We aren't talking about the kind of silence where you consciously set aside time for it for a few minutes a day through meditation or such other mindfulness practices. We are talking about incorporating silence in your routine 'throughout the day', which essentially means to start speaking less in general. You need to reduce your quantity of speech overall during the day across most of your conversations. Being quiet for a few minutes in the morning and then talking excessively and restlessly for the rest of your day does no good to your goal of becoming more peaceful in the long term. This is like respecting your mother only on Mother's Day or caring for your partner only on your anniversary.

Contemplation on the Adios principles in silence for a few minutes, spending time in deep thought, taking a quiet walk outside, finding a quiet corner in your home to reflect or reducing your interactions with technology are all good habits and will serve you well. But silence needs to permeate the fabric of your entire day for you to feel its true impact. You need to feel it, not understand it intellectually.

In an always-on world that encourages constant noise and instant communication, adding regular silence to your routine is even more important. By inserting moments of silence in your life, you can tap into its power and experience the peace and clarity it brings.

Speaking too much can create a sense of restlessness within you. When your mind is constantly occupied with words, there is little space for stillness and reflection. The constant need to talk to fill the silence can leave you feeling drained and over-whelmed. Adding silence to speech allows you to recharge and find a sense of inner calm.

If you speak a lot, it might be because of various reasons. Some-times, it could be due to a fear of awkwardness or discomfort that silence can bring. You may feel the need to keep the conver-sation flowing. It might create a kind of psychological pressure to say something, anything, because you have come to believe that if two or more people get together, they have to talk constantly. So, you might talk a lot more than necessary and may also rush to fill any silent gaps in the interaction with filler words such as 'umm'. It's almost like staying silent even for a short duration is some sort of sin.

In other instances, it could stem from a desire to be heard, validated, or to assert your presence in a group.

Let's say you are participating in a group discussion at school or work. You might notice that whenever there is a moment of silence, you feel compelled to speak up and share your thoughts, even if you don't have anything substantial to contribute. You may fear being seen as disengaged or worry that others might think less of you if you remain silent. As a result, you continuously fill the space with unnecessary views, elaborations, or repetitions. You speak for the sake of speaking, not because you have something meaningful to say. You speak to get rid of the silence. You might actively try to find things to say that make you look smart. If there is silence during the conversation, you might feel restless and look at others around you hoping that someone will fill that void and begin to feel uncomfortable beyond a point if no one rises to the occasion.

You might find yourself constantly talking in social gatherings or parties. Perhaps you feel the need to appear confident or interesting, so you continuously share stories and experiences. This excessive speech can leave you feeling drained because you are expending a lot of energy trying to keep up with the conversation and maintain a certain image.

The constant need to talk merely to fill the silence can also leave you feeling more restless. It can prevent you from finding moments of stillness and Contemplation, which are essential for your overall well-being. By speaking less overall during the day, you can recharge and find inner calm. Taking breaks from constant speaking gives your mind a chance to rest, process information, and regain focus.

During a work presentation, you might feel the urge to over-explain your ideas and keep talking even after conveying your message, fearing that silence might imply a lack of preparation or competence.

In an argument with a friend or family member, you may feel compelled to keep defending your viewpoint, constantly interjecting and interrupting, which only fuels the conflict further.

Deleting words from your speech enables you to recharge, create space for Contemplation and gain deeper clarity. Business owners and CEOs who have gone through the Adios program have said that speaking less and slower allowed them to think a lot more cohesively, present their ideas more convincingly and confidently while feeling more peaceful internally. Certain parents found that speaking less not only reduced their own stress on a day-to-day basis but also improved their relationship with their teenage children, and in some cases inspired their children to become calmer, less irritable and more mature. They stopped scoffing at every small thing and started to become more polite and respectful.

Try it today. Do it for at least three weeks and see how you feel.

Speaking a lot generally reduces your own peace of mind, and it significantly obstructs your journey of self-knowledge. However, it can also have other negative consequences that affect both yourself and others.

Let's say you're in a group of friends, and someone shares a personal story with you in confidence. However, you casually share that story with others without their permission. Just because you are habituated to speaking a lot, when you were sitting with those other friends, you felt compelled to talk about something, and that story came to mind. Not only does this breach the trust your friend placed in you, but it also creates a negative environment where people might feel unsafe sharing their sensitive personal experiences with you in the future.

Words have the power to uplift or hurt others. When you speak without being thoughtful, you may unintentionally make hurtful or offensive remarks that can deeply impact someone's feelings.

Insensitive jokes, derogatory comments, or thoughtless criticism can be emotionally damaging to some people.

For example, suppose you're speaking with a colleague who is struggling with a particular project. Without considering their feelings, you make a joke about their abilities. Your words may deeply hurt them, causing embarrassment, and diminishing their self-esteem. All this just because you did not have control over how much to speak.

In a heated argument, inserting a moment of silence instead of impulsively reacting can defuse tension and allow both parties to calm down. It provides an opportunity to reflect on the situation and choose words thoughtfully. Speaking less will also help you remove words that could hurt the other person. Just cut them out. Be silent instead.

In personal relationships, moments of silence allow you to be meaningful and intimate. Sharing a comfortable silence with your significant other can convey a sense of deep love and companionship, strengthening the bond you share. Yes, chatting away and silly jokes also have an important place to keep the bond strong, but do not underestimate the importance of silence to deepen love in an intimate relationship. Similarly, in a situation where you have a disagreement, your ability to control your speech can do you a lot of good to ensure the situation doesn't get out of hand.

The primary reason to speak less is to enhance your ability of self-reflection and Contemplation so you improve your own clarity of thought and peace of mind. Speaking less is extremely good for your peace of mind.

A social media channel whose entire business model depends on you speaking all the time may encourage you to speak more and more. But your well-being isn't their responsibility. Your well-being is your responsibility. They don't discuss your peace of mind in their team meetings. Your peace of mind isn't their priority. But the question is - Is it your priority?

Also, what about freedom of speech?

Freedom of speech is a cornerstone of democratic societies, granting individuals the right to express their thoughts and ideas. It enables open dialogue, encourages diverse perspectives to be heard, and has the power to drive positive change. However, freedom of speech is a right. You need to exercise that right thoughtfully.

Freedom of speech does not imply talking incessantly. Just because you are free to talk all the time doesn't mean you must talk all the time. Just because you have the right to free speech doesn't mean you must exercise it every minute.

In today's world, both in-person and online environments often encourage a culture of constant communication. A talkative environment can push you to keep speaking without purpose or intention. In the excitement to fit in or gain attention, you may find yourself engaging in trivial discussions that waste your time and attention and also reduce your peace of mind. Valuable moments that could be spent pursuing matters that matter are often lost in the sea of unimportant chatter.

Continuous talking has a profound impact on your inner state. It can make you more restless and insecure, constantly seeking validation or approval through your words. In the pursuit of constantly keeping up with the conversation, you may find yourself focusing on how to talk about a meaningful personal event in an interesting manner, rather than genuinely experiencing and enjoying that event in that moment. This preoccupation with presentation and performance to impress others leads to a shallow existence, which will reduce your sense of meaning and purpose in life, leading to feeling less peaceful within.

Imagine a mother, Janet, who is taking her child, Lily, to the park. They are surrounded by the vibrant colors of nature, the laughter of other children, and the warmth of the sun. Lily is excitedly exploring the playground, calling out to her mother to watch her climb, swing, and slide.

However, Janet's mind is preoccupied with thoughts of sharing this experience on social media. She pulls out her phone, eager to capture the perfect video that will impress her online audience. She starts to think about what caption would best describe the moment, how to frame the video to make it more appealing, and what hashtags will attract more likes and comments.

Lost in this digital world, Janet becomes more focused on crafting a superficial connection with an unknown audience than on fully immersing herself in the present moment with her own child. While Lily looks up at her, seeking attention and a smile from her mother, Janet remains glued to her phone and loses the moment she could have spent with her daughter, a moment that will never return.

Instead of being fully present as a mother, Janet becomes disconnected and distant. This happens often at home too and eventually, Lily grows up as an insecure child, constantly snapping at small matters and scoffing or rolling her eyes at petty things. Because her mother was too busy impressing strangers rather than being there for her, Lily is unable to develop a strong emotional connection with Janet.

An emotional connection needs two people. If one of them is missing, the connection isn't complete. In this case, Janet was unavailable mentally and emotionally even though she was present there physically. Instead of focusing on what might make Lily's life more fulfilled and peaceful, Janet was busy indulging in trivial speech with people who may not have mattered as much. So the connection between her and her daughter was never complete.

While freedom of speech is vital for a thriving society, it is equally important to recognize the value of silence to create a more fulfilling, purposeful, and peaceful life for yourself. Continuously speaking without purpose or reflection can divert your attention from what truly matters and leave you feeling restless and insecure. By adopting a fair measure of silence during the day as a lifestyle and valuing quality over quantity in conversations, you can cultivate a deeper sense of fulfillment and feel more meaningful and peaceful.

Just like you have the right to speak, you also have the right to remain silent. The question is - do you have the ability?

In our society, there exists a common misconception that speaking a lot equals being intelligent and knowledgeable. Many people believe that the more words they utter, the more credible and wiser they appear to others. We often come across individuals who dominate discussions with a barrage of words, overwhelming others with their seemingly vast knowledge. They speak confidently and assertively, leaving little room for others to contribute. Consequently, they are praised and deemed as the brightest in the room.

True intelligence lies not in the quantity, but in the quality of one's words. A person who speaks incessantly may sometimes possess only a superficial understanding of a topic, relying on memorized facts and shallow information. They may lack the ability to engage in critical thinking or consider multiple perspectives. In contrast, a person who speaks thoughtfully and concisely, choosing their words carefully, often demonstrates a deeper understanding and a genuine grasp of the subject matter.

Even when you possess a wealth of knowledge and substance about your material, the addition of silence to your speech will greatly enhance your communication. When you speak less but more thoughtfully, you feel more confident and more peaceful.

You can also be more articulate about your topic and get your point across more clearly.

A knowledgeable speaker may lecture for hours, sharing their expertise on a subject matter at a workshop. While their vast knowledge may be evident, incorporating moments of silence into their presentation can greatly benefit the audience. Silence allows individuals to process information, reflect on the content, and connect it with their existing knowledge to enhance their understanding.

In professional settings, meetings can often turn into verbal battlegrounds where individuals vie for dominance through their verbosity. Those who speak the most may be seen as assertive and influential, but their constant stream of words may stifle collaboration and discourage others from putting forth their ideas during the meeting. It can also be demoralizing for other employees if such behavior starts to become the basis for professional growth through promotions or pay raises.

True innovation is possible only when individuals speak less, take some time out for individual Contemplation on their own, listen to others attentively during group discussions rather than waiting for the other person to stop speaking so they can put forth their own point of view, respect one another's perspectives, and offer thoughtful contributions. This combination of individual Contemplation sessions and thoughtful group discussion can start to produce innovation at will, whenever you want, in whichever area you want. Adding Contemplation to the mix can make innovation predictable and repeatable, quarter on quarter. Imagine what that could do to an organization where innovation could change fortunes.

There is an emphasis on public speaking skills nowadays. While public speaking is about "speaking" in public, it is not about speaking as much as possible. If you want to take your public speaking to the next level, aim to speak less. Don't speak to prove you are clever or to impress others. Speak less but speak impactfully and with conviction. Contemplation helps you develop that conviction. Speak only when your words add more value than your silence.

In personal relationships, the addition of silence can be particularly transformative in some cases. Imagine yourself engaged in a heated argument with your partner, each vying to make their point heard. By recognizing the importance of silence, you can pause, take a breath, and listen to one another. In that silence, you may be able to truly understand each other's perspectives and reach a resolution that considers both your needs.

As I mentioned earlier, the primary reason to reduce your quantity of speech and add silence in most of your conversations is for your own growth on the path of self-knowledge and living a more peaceful life. Excessive speech obstructs Contemplation and self-reflection. It tends to increase your restlessness and reduce your peace of mind.

In a world inundated with noise and distractions, silence allows you to turn inward, listen to the various voices in your mind, and choose the one that makes you feel more fulfilled, purposeful, and peaceful. Silence enables you to deepen your understanding of yourself and make decisions that are aligned with your inner peace. You can hear yourself better.

Speaking less does not mean that you refrain from speaking up for yourself when it is truly necessary in personal or professional settings. Putting a firm point across can be done thoughtfully and effectively, while also maintaining your peace of mind.

When you choose to speak less, it means being selective and intentional with your words. It's about understanding the value of silence and using it strategically to make your voice more impactful where necessary while maintaining your inner peace of mind. Think of silence as another phrase you use in your conversation, a phrase with no words. When asserting something, instead of engaging in long arguments, practice expressing yourself using fewer words in a clear, concise, and respectful manner.

You can also use your speech to set boundaries with others. Setting boundaries in your intimate relationships can sometimes give you a sense of empowerment and control over your own life. However, focusing solely on what you want and being overly individualistic at the expense of your partner can also damage the love and connection in your relationship, and eventually your own peace of mind.

While setting boundaries is about defining personal limits and needs, it should not be an excuse to be rude or dismissive toward your partner. Relationships thrive on love, respect, and care. By communicating your preferences in a loving, thoughtful and respectful manner, without ever using the word 'boundaries', you can maintain the balance between your preferences and the emotional connection with your partner.

Also be careful about the people who are generally angry about relationships and focus too much on what they want rather than on creating a healthy, loving relationship. Many of them wear the mask of empowerment but beneath that mask, their own life tends to be broken, unfulfilled and lacks inner peace. Their advice might lead you in a similar direction. Ask yourself - What will make me more fulfilled and peaceful? What might feel good in the short term but may not feel peaceful in the long run? - and use your practice of Contemplation on these questions to make your decision yourself.

Drawing unnecessary dividers and being impolite may feel good and empowering in the moment, but it usually leads to strained relationships and eventually a loss of warmth with your partner.

The bridges of love are fragile. Don't burn them in the enthusiasm of setting rigid boundaries. Sometimes, a warm conversation is all you need.

In professional settings, speaking less but thoughtfully can contribute to your professional growth and success. It is about finding the balance between actively participating in discussions and meetings, and using silence strategically to listen, observe, and reflect. When you do speak, make sure your words are clear and contribute meaningfully to the conversation. Stay away from speaking for the sake of breaking the silence in the room or to get noticed by others even when you have nothing meaningful to say.

If you believe you are at an organization that values and rewards people who speak for the sake of speaking rather than valuing meaningful speech, change your organization, not your personality or values. Find a new job but retain your peace of mind. If it's a rat race, choose to remain human. It might be difficult in the short run, but you will thank yourself in the long run. Remember to ask - Does this culture make me more peaceful or less peaceful?

By speaking less, you can protect your peace of mind and maintain a sense of inner calm. Speaking less allows you to avoid unnecessary stress, conflicts, and misunderstandings that can arise from impulsive or excessive speech. Silence allows you to focus on what truly matters and allocate your energy where it is most needed.

Speech is a tool for communication. Use it for that purpose. Speak to improve and maintain your peace of mind. Speak for the right reasons. If, however, you speak not because you have something meaningful to say but because you do not have the ability to remain silent, that is not communication. That is an addiction, the same as drug or alcohol addiction. If not doing something creates physical restlessness and unease in your body, it is an addiction. If you are compulsively committed or helplessly drawn to doing something, it is an addiction. If you are unable to stop engaging in a behavior that is harmful for you, it is an addiction. So, ask yourself - is your speech a communication tool in your life or is it an addiction? When you are with other people, do you speak because you feel uncomfortable being silent or are you quite comfortable being silent and speaking only when you need to?

Speaking less will do you a lot of good. Try it for three weeks and see how you feel.

In which dimensions of your life today can you apply the principle of Quantity of Speech?

_____

_____

_____

CHAPTER TAKEAWAYS:

- How much you speak directly impacts your peace of mind. If you speak a lot, you tend to be more restless.
- Speaking less throughout the day is important. Reduce your words in most conversations during the day.
- If you wish to make serious progress in your self-knowledge journey, speaking less is a must.
- Adding more silence helps you think better and speak thoughtfully. It can also help you express yourself more clearly.
- Speak only if your words can add more value than your silence. Don't speak for the sake of speaking or filling up the silence in the room.

- Speech should be a tool to say something meaningful. It should not be an addiction. You should be comfortable staying silent when you are with others.
- Speaking less can increase your peace of mind to a large extent.

~

15. PRINCIPLE TEN: VELOCITY, PITCH AND VOLUME OF SPEECH

Apart from the quality and quantity of your speech, its speed, pitch, and volume also make a tremendous impact on your peace of mind.

Speaking fast usually makes you more restless. You might feel a sense of urgency to convey things quickly, but if you slow down your speech, not only will you be able to communicate more clearly, but you will also feel more peaceful within.

Very often, you tend to speak fast because of the environment around you - many people around you - speak fast and that puts subconscious pressure on you to level up. But the societal pressure to speak fast often leads to superficial conversations.

Speaking fast leaves little room for reflection and introspection. It becomes challenging to fully grasp the significance of your words and their potential impact on your own mind and on others. By adopting a slower pace, you can pause, reflect, and choose your words wisely. This improves your inner peace and your communication with others.

In a world filled with constant noise and distractions, speaking a lot and speaking fast may be seen as a way to assert yourself and be heard. However, the quantity or velocity of your words does not always equal their value. By practicing speaking slower, you can cut through the noise and focus on conveying your thoughts and ideas with clarity and purpose.

You have the power to either create inner peace through your speech, or to destroy it. The words you choose and the way you express them have a profound impact on how you feel within. When you speak gently, with softness and calmness, you tend to feel calmer and more peaceful within. In some cases, you also influence others to be calmer and more peaceful.

Your speech is like a mirror reflecting your emotions. If you are agitated from the inside, it might reflect in the way you speak. Fortunately, the reverse is also true. When you speak softly and calmly, it allows you to create a calm environment within you so you can navigate through life's challenges with grace and composure. By choosing gentle words and a warm tone, you create a positive internal environment within yourself.

By speaking softly and calmly, you also create an atmosphere of friendliness and warmth for those around you.

Speaking slowly, softly, and calmly has the power to transform your inner landscape. It helps to quiet the noise and chaos within your mind. By using a gentle tone and speaking at a slow pace, you maintain a certain stillness within you. That stillness is very powerful. You need that stillness to live a peaceful life.

When you speak softly, you allow your words to flow gracefully. This not only brings a sense of peace to your own being but also creates a soothing effect on those who hear you. It is common to observe similar effects on the people who are around you. They may not instantly change but very often, you will learn that they tend to feel more peaceful around you. That is because you are projecting your inner peace outside through your speech.

Try speaking at a slow pace - 50% slower if you speak not-so-slowly today - during your next few conversations at home, work and in social situations for the next seven days. How do you feel? It might feel a little difficult, even odd, at first because it might be unfamiliar. But once you get used to it, ask yourself how it feels - more peaceful or less peaceful?

Adios members who were accustomed to speaking fast because of their environment have experienced profound changes in their personality, and in some cases, have been able to redefine the future trajectory of their life. Just because speaking slowly gave them a glimpse into a whole new person inside of them, a clearer, calmer person. Once you taste that, you don't want to go back.

Do not take your speech lightly. You might speak a lot during the day, and that makes it an important lever to maintain, or take away, your peace of mind.

In moments of conflict, your choice, tone and pace of words can make an especially significant difference. Gentle speech can defuse tension and create a friendlier or at least less hostile environment suitable for understanding and resolution. By speaking softly and calmly, you can navigate through conflicts with grace and calmness.

Instead of escalating the conflict with harsh words or a raised voice, choose gentleness as your style. Think about someone who is angry and shouting. By responding to them in a loud, angry tone, will you calm them down or further worsen the problem? Soft-spoken words can disarm anger and hostility and encourage others to relax as well. It will help you avoid aggravating the situation further. Through gentle speech, you might also be able to encourage the other person to express their thoughts and emotions more openly and without fear, which helps them feel heard due to which they might be open to calming down.

Think about a delayed flight situation with the customers getting agitated. While the ground staff might be able to do little about the flight delay, the best they can do is stay calm, attend to the angry customers politely and be kind and helpful. It won't take very long for the situation to get dangerously out of hand if they too start replying to those passengers in a loud angry voice. Sometimes, you might feel that their calm voice isn't really doing much because the passengers are yelling anyways but think about what their angry voice would do in that situation. Not letting hostility get out of hand is equally important, even if it is invisible to the naked eye.

Why might you speak in a high pitch or raise your voice?

Emotions play a significant role in how you communicate, and they can influence your speech patterns. When you experience intense emotions such as excitement, anger, or frustration, it is natural for your voice to reflect those emotions. In such moments, speaking at a high pitch or loudly may be a natural response to the intensity of our feelings.

Pay attention to what it does to you when expressing intense emotions through speech. While it is healthy to let your emotions be heard, it is equally important to consider the impact of your words on your own peace of mind and that of others around you. Speaking in a high pitch or loudly can reduce your inner peace and also negatively impact important relationships.

It is believed that a louder or more intense speech can help convey a sense of power and command attention. In some cases, such speech patterns may be seen as a sign of confidence and assertiveness.

However, it is essential to recognize that assertiveness and authority should not solely rely on the volume or pitch of your voice. True assertiveness involves expressing your thoughts in a clear, calm and respectful manner, with conviction but without negativity.

It is very easy to give in to anger or speak disrespectfully to someone. But the real power lies in being able to control it and eliminate it from your personality. Speaking in a high pitch or volume may also create a temporary impression of authority, but it may not lead to long-term peace of mind or respect.

You might also sometimes raise your voice to make up for the lack of clarity in your own mind. If you are clear and have a strong mind, you can convey your thoughts in a calm and composed tone without resorting to high pitch or excessive volume. This keeps you more peaceful and also builds a healthy external environment where ideas can be discussed in a friendly manner.

When it comes to public speaking or performing, using high pitch and volume can be a strategic way to capture attention and create impact. The human ear is naturally drawn to sounds that are louder or higher in pitch, which can help to immediately grab the audience's attention and make a memorable impression.

But do not underestimate the power of calm and composed speech during public speaking. Just because someone is louder does not mean they are necessarily better or superior. With some practice, you can make your point confidently, and in some cases more impactfully, by speaking at a slow pace in a calm and composed tone.

If you wish to take your public speaking to the next level, add silence to it. Try speaking less, at a slower pace and in a calmer tone.

Speech patterns, including preferences for pitch and volume, can be significantly influenced by environmental factors. If you spend a lot of time in an environment where most people speak very loudly (or too much or too fast), you might also tend to do the same without even realizing you are doing so.

Your goal is to create a more fulfilled and peaceful life, so you need to constantly ask yourself - Is this making me more peaceful or is it making me more restless / less peaceful? What are the usual or most frequent environments in your life today? Do they encourage you to speak too much, or fast? Are they making you more restless?

To adopt the habit of speaking slowly and softly, think about how your day was, whether you spoke too much, too fast, or loudly, and then practice speaking slowly and softly. Notice the pace and tone you normally use to communicate. Take moments throughout the day to consciously slow down and soften your voice. Practice remaining silent often during conversations, allowing others to speak without interrupting them or rushing to respond. Use regular pauses to reflect on what is going on in the conversation and choose your words cautiously.

Fast speech very often increases restlessness. Fast is usually restless.

Slow your speech down deliberately and considerably until you can hear and feel a conspicuous difference. Just a little slower may not have adequate impact. If you feel awkward or uncomfortable, it means you are doing it right.

Try it with your work-related conversations as well as your personal conversations, but do it consciously - first practice alone, on your own, to reduce your speed considerably by repeating 4-5 sentences at a really slow pace at least ten times. Then remind yourself before you start to speak to someone and speak considerably slowly during that conversation.

If you are habitually a fast speaker, this might take some time. You might find it a little difficult because your body is unfamiliar with the slower pace. You just need to keep at it. No rush. Do it for a few days and ask yourself - Is this helping me? Does this make me feel more peaceful?

Don't worry about how you appear to others. Focus on how you feel.

Try it out a few times and judge for yourself. Don't believe me. Be a scientist. Experiment yourself and see how it feels. You decide what is right for you in your life.

In which dimensions of your life today can you apply the ADIOS principle of Velocity, Pitch & Volume of Speech?

_____

_____

_____

CHAPTER TAKEAWAYS:

- Speaking slowly can reduce your restlessness and improve your peace of mind.
- Speaking in a softer tone in a calm and composed manner enhances your inner peace.
- Faster and louder are not necessarily better.
- Slowing down your speech helps you think and express yourself more clearly.
- Speaking in a calm and composed manner can help you handle challenging conversations more effectively.

16. PRINCIPLE ELEVEN: LOOKING INSIDE VS OUTSIDE

It's quite common and natural to seek validation and recognition from the world around us. We want to be acknowledged for our achievements, accepted by our peers, and praised for our efforts. The world around you also tends to reward praise and attention disproportionately. And that is exactly what you need to be careful about. Everything that feels good may not necessarily be right for you in the long run. It may not bring long term peace of mind.

When you rely on external validation, you place your happiness and fulfillment in the hands of others. You seek approval and recognition as a measure of your success, believing that your worth is defined by what you achieve or how others perceive you. But this constant need for validation can leave you feeling empty and unfulfilled, always chasing the next accomplishment or reward.

This is called the Look Syndrome, where your mind is constantly saying: Look at me, look how talented I am, look how clever I am, etc. This tends to increase your restlessness and reduce your peace of mind.

Society often emphasizes external achievements, fame, and material possessions as markers of success. We are bombarded with messages that tell us we need to be the best, have the most, and always be one step ahead. This creates a pressure to constantly prove ourselves and seek validation from others.

However, your worth is not determined by external factors, even though the external noise might suggest that it is. Your value lies in your unique qualities, your character, and your intrinsic worth as a human being. Keeping your focus inward rather than outward is the best way to keep your mind peaceful.

Since you are kids, you get the message that success equals stuff - the better grades, the fancier job titles, the nicer cars and houses. Society makes it seem like you have to have all that to be a winner. And if you don't check those boxes, people look down on you.

It's easy to start thinking you need applause and trophies from others to feel good about yourself. To base your worth on what you can put on your resume or show off on social media. Society might say that is how success looks like, and they want you to chase that as well because somewhere deep down, it makes them feel they are doing the right thing too.

But that kind of thinking makes you chase cardboard cutouts of achievement without thinking about what really makes you fulfilled and peaceful. Some life script handed to you by society isn't usually the best script for you, because it isn't your script. It is someone else's.

You have to tune that noise out. Decide for yourself what success really looks like in your own life. Find out what will make you feel fulfilled, what work will bring meaning and purpose to your life, what kind of partner will make you feel peaceful. Find those answers yourself using Contemplation. Look inward, not outward.

Media and advertising regularly contribute to this culture of seeking external validation. You are constantly exposed to images and messages that suggest happiness and fulfillment can be attained through material things, popularity, and social status. This constant exposure can create a sense of pressure, and sometimes a habit, to seek validation through external means.

Social comparison plays a significant role in reinforcing the importance of external achievements. You often negatively compare yourself to others (Check the chapter on Negative Comparison), measuring your success and worth based on how you measure up against societal standards or the accomplishments of your parents, siblings, cousins, friends, peers or even strangers.

In certain cultures, or families, there can be intense pressure to meet societal expectations. The fear of judgment and the desire to fit in can lead you to focus on external achievements and seek validation from your community, rather than focusing on what feels right to you.

If everyone around you is talking about it, it is hard to block out that noise and listen to your voice within, the voice that wants you to be more peaceful. That is where Contemplation helps you.

A unanimous decision is just a unanimous decision. It is not necessarily the right decision. Just because many people around you are following a particular path doesn't automatically mean that it is right for you as well. By practicing regular Contemplation, you can create a deeper connection with yourself and discover what is really right for you - what makes you more fulfilled and peaceful. Only you can decide that. No one else can.

Relying solely on external validation for happiness and fulfillment can have serious consequences on your well-being. When your sense of self-worth is dependent on the opinions and approval of others, you give away your power and control over your own happiness to others. When your mind focuses on looking good in the eyes of others, you tend to forget who you really are.

A constant need for validation creates a never-ending cycle of seeking approval and recognition. You may find yourself constantly striving for more achievements, possessions, or praise in order to feel validated. This pursuit can be exhausting, and ultimately unsatisfying, as external validation is often short-lived and tends to eventually leave you less peaceful in the end.

It can also negatively affect your self-worth. If you base your happiness on the approval of others, you are vulnerable to feeling unworthy when that validation is not received. You are waiting for someone else to tell you that you are good enough rather than looking within and judging that on your own. Your self-esteem may suffer, and you may question your own abilities, which can reduce your peace of mind and keep you anxious.

Additionally, relying on external validation can encourage you to be less honest. When your focus is solely on meeting the expectations of others, or impressing or pleasing others, you may sacrifice your true self and your core values in the excitement of receiving something that might be short-lived. You may say or do things that don't truly reflect who you really are.

A blind pursuit of external validation can affect your personal growth and not allow you to maximize your true potential. It may distract you from being able to live your own story. Instead of exploring your own interests, strengths, and passions, you may be driven by the desire to impress others or gain their approval by doing what might impress them.

For example, an artist might become so fascinated by something that looks fancier and more popular that she may completely ignore what she really stands for, what she is naturally good at and what makes her who she is. A corporate leader might focus so much on what their competition is doing that they may not devote sufficient time and attention to finding their own uniqueness that can help them position differently in the extremely crowded market. That unique positioning is waiting to be discovered inside your heads, but your team needs a systematic process of Contemplation to find it. Only group brainstorming won't do.

Focusing only outward can also limit your individual potential and prevent you from fully exploring your own unique talents and creativity. Imitating others blindly might bring material success, but it may also leave you feeling hollow from the inside. That is because you generate self-worth by going deep within yourself, finding who you are and living your own story, not someone else's.

Ultimately, relying unduly on external validation for happiness and fulfillment can leave you feeling empty, unfulfilled, and restless.

Spending a few minutes in Contemplation to find yourself will help you a lot. It will help you think clearly about what you must do and why, to understand what makes you you and will make you feel fulfilled, purposeful, and peaceful. This will help you resist the external temptations that might distract you from your own unique path.

Reconnecting with your own values and your personal non-financial vision is a vital step in this process. Use Contemplation to reflect on what truly brings you fulfillment and peace, independent of external appreciation. What activities, hobbies, or causes ignite a fire within you? What makes every cell in your body say - Yes this is who I am. By using Contemplation to tune into your inner voices, find the voice that will help you live a more fulfilling and purposeful life. It is there. You just need to tune in and listen carefully.

Contemplation helps you understand all aspects of yourself, including your strengths, weaknesses, quirks, and imperfections. It helps you recognize that you are a unique individual with your own set of motivations, experiences, and talents. It helps you create a deep connection with yourself, so you know who you really are, what really matters to you, what makes you more fulfilled and peaceful and what doesn't.

You must live your own story. Jason's story might be about building roads and bridges. John's story might be to run a bakery or a restaurant. Emily's story might be to fight for social justice. Sarah's story might be to understand nature intricately. Joe's story might be about taking care of his parents. Jane's story might be to raise her children well. My story is to train people in Contemplation to help them improve their clarity of thought and peace of mind.

What's your story?

It doesn't have to sound profound or save the world, because both of these are again usually measured by how many people in the external world appreciate it. It should just be yours. Personal. Intimate. Yours. That's what matters.

By deeply understanding, accepting, and appreciating who you are, you create a foundation of self-worth that is not dependent on external validation. It starts with you understanding yourself deeply for which you need to spend time with yourself, talking to yourself without any bias, in silence. A Dialogue In Objective Silence (ADIOS). Just the two of you - you and yourself.

If you regularly spend time in Contemplation, thinking deeply about matters that matter to you, you will find clarity and deeper insights about them. If you wish to share these ideas with others, you can express yourself genuinely and without fear of judgment because you have thought deeply about them and you know you believe in what you are saying. This does not mean that others won't judge you. Many might judge, criticize, or even reject your views. That is where your conviction about your thoughts comes in.

If you spend sufficient time in Contemplation connecting with yourself, you will find that you not only have clarity but also have the courage to stick to what you believe in despite external judgment and criticism. You will seek long-term peace by doing or saying what you believe in rather than doing what you may not believe in but provides short-term validation or money, or doing something merely because many people around you are doing it. This also helps you attract people who resonate with you and build deeper relationships.

When you focus too much on external appearances and seek others' attention or appreciation through them, you run the risk of reducing your inner peace.

For example, consider a romantic relationship where partners focus on projecting an idealized image of their bond to the outside world rather than building and maintaining genuine emotional connection between themselves. They may constantly present a flawless facade to the outside world, sharing picture-perfect moments and showering each other with lavish gifts. However, behind closed doors, they may struggle with communication issues, lack of emotional support, insecurity, or a sense of disconnection. They may lack the basic ingredients of such a relationship - care, attention, love, and respect. They may say all the right things, but the essence might be missing. That's sometimes because they are focusing too much on speaking or maintaining appearances and less on whether they feel peaceful and fulfilled with each other. The focus on the external can take their focus away from the essence of their relationship.

Since this external validation provides only short-term happiness, they need to constantly engage in that behavior, leading to further restlessness and reduction of peace of mind. This is a kind of psychological addiction where your drug is attention, praise, or appreciation from others.

In the workplace, individuals may feel compelled to constantly showcase their achievements, skills, and professional successes to impress their bosses and peers. This can create an unhealthy competitive environment where genuine collaboration and support take a backseat. Rather than building relationships based on mutual respect, cooperation, and shared goals, the focus shifts to outshining or impressing others to receive rewards or promotions.

In the dating world, individuals may present an idealized version of themselves to attract potential partners. They may emphasize their physical appearance, material possessions, or social status as a way to gain validation and attention. If you focus too much on these aspects, you might miss the fundamental factors that are necessary to make a relationship fulfilling and meaningful in the long-term.

If your relationship rests on a weak foundation, cracks very often appear sooner or later. If, on the other hand, you took your time to look inward to know yourself deeply and consider what kind of partner would make you feel more fulfilled and peaceful, you are more likely to find the right person because you are looking for something specific rather than being distracted or impressed by external appearances alone.

When it comes to dating, use the following Adios approach: Find Yourself. Find a Friend. Find a Partner. In that order. Contemplation on the Adios principles help you understand yourself better and in turn also understand the kind of person you would like to be with and why. It will also help you define the characteristics that you don't want in your partner.

When you constantly seek validation from others, you become trapped in a cycle where your self-esteem rises and falls based on external validation. This cycle creates a constant sense of rest-lessness, as you are always seeking the next accomplishment, recognition, or praise to temporarily fill the void within yourself.

While external validation may provide fleeting moments of satis-faction, it often leaves you yearning for more. You chase after external markers of success, hoping they will bring you lasting fulfillment. However, true fulfillment comes from knowing your-self well, from aligning your actions with what makes you feel more peaceful, finding meaning in your own journey and living your own story. The more you rely on external praise, the further you move away from discovering yourself and the peace that comes with it.

The restlessness that stems from seeking constant external vali-dation can lead to feelings of insecurity, anxiety, and a constant need for attention from others, which can erode your peace of mind. You may find yourself constantly comparing yourself to others, feeling inadequate, or trapped in a never-ending cycle of seeking approval. You are good enough only if someone else says you are good enough. You may also tend to become more irritable and in general live in a constant state of insecurity.

Contemplation on the Adios principles helps you break free from this restlessness. It enables you to cultivate self-awareness and achieve clarity of thought which helps you clearly see what makes you more peaceful and what takes away your peace of mind. Contemplation helps you connect with your internal sources of validation and maintain that connection on an ongoing basis.

By focusing on your values and your own non-financial vision for your life, you gain a higher amount of self-acceptance and understand that you are unique and have your own story to live. You don't need to exhibit that story to the world for their approval. This clarity helps you find a sense of fulfillment that is not dependent on someone else and is also not short-lived or fleeting.

Look inward to find your clarity, your peace and your story. The external world will adjust itself accordingly.

In which dimensions of your life today can you apply the ADIOS principle of Looking Inside vs Outside?

_____

_____

_____

TINA'S ADIOSCOPE

Situation

I've loved being a stay-at-home mom, but now I want to return to work too. As much as it pains me to leave my young son Jeremy, it's time to find balance between being a mom and pursuing my own goals again. I worry how this big change will impact him and our close bond. But I know I need to do what's right for both of us.

Twin Voices:

Voice 1 says: You should go back to work. It will provide financial stability for you and Jeremy. You'll have a fulfilling career. Plus, Jeremy will benefit from interacting with other children in daycare.

Voice 2 says: Spending more time with Jeremy at home is crucial. These early years are precious, and you don't want to miss out on his milestones. You can provide him with a loving and nurturing environment, being there for him every step of the way.

If I follow Voice 1 and go back to work, I might find fulfillment in my career and financial stability. However, there might be a lingering sense of guilt at important moments with Jeremy. But if I chose Voice 2 and focus on spending more time at home, I might experience joy in seeing Jeremy's growth and being his primary caregiver. Yet, there could be concerns about financial strain or potential career stagnation.

Looking inside vs outside

I do get affected by what I see around me. When I see other women earning well and going on luxurious holidays, it does pinch me that I am unable to do that even though I am quite capable of earning well. But I also understand that Jeremy needs me right now so sacrificing my work is for a reason that is much more important in the long run. These days will never come back.

But I know I will feel frustrated if I do not pursue my professional dreams because they mean a lot to me as well. I think what will make me peaceful is waiting for another year or so and being with my son at home but starting to take up part-time work during this time so I can get warmed up and then hopefully I can go full-time in a year or two. This will ensure that I don't ignore my son and also not ignore my career.

I want to start working now, even if it is part-time, because I am clearly starting to get a little uncomfortable about being out of a job for some time. This isn't just about comparing myself with those other women or not being able to make money so I can spend it on things I love. I also want to be active professionally, because it gives me a lot of satisfaction. I don't want to end up frustrated in the future.

Starting to work part-time will keep me peaceful on the professional front because I would have begun my professional journey again. This will also allow me to be with Jeremy at home, which will keep me peaceful on the personal front.

SHAWN'S ADIOSCOPE

Situation

My girlfriend keeps pressuring me to get engaged after four years together. This morning when she brought it up again over breakfast, I tried to dodge the topic with small talk. But the tension remained. She stared at me eagerly, waiting for the answer she wanted to hear. I feel uneasy.

Twin Voices:

One voice warns me of potentially losing freedom and independence that may go along with marriage. It reminds me of the importance of maintaining my individuality and the uncertainties that lie ahead.

The other voice nudges me to consider the benefits of a committed partnership. It emphasizes the importance of building a future together with Helen, whom I love a lot, creating a sense of warmth and stability.

Voice 1 cautions me about the potential risks and sacrifices I may have to make. Will I feel trapped in a commitment I'm not fully prepared for? Voice 2 reminds me of the love and connection I share with Helen, the joy we've experienced together, and the joys of support in a marriage.

One voice says that finding purpose and fulfillment in my career can be enough. The other voice argues that building a life with Helen can offer a different kind of fulfillment, one with love, companionship, and shared experiences, something that my work alone can never offer.

Looking inside vs outside

I tend to care a lot about what others think of me and how I am perceived by others in the world. I feel the urge to prove myself, especially when it comes to my relationship with Helen. I'm afraid of disappointing her or not living up to her expectations. This dependence on her validation and the idea of marriage has created a sense of restlessness within me, as my happiness seems to rely heavily on meeting these external standards.

I also look at other couples with kids and see how happy they look and wonder if I am missing out on those joys of life. I would love to be a father and a good friend to my sons and daughters.

But when I look inside, I feel a sense of restlessness, a kind of incompleteness within me, which is holding me back from being happy about getting engaged to Helen. Yes, it has been a long time together and I love her deeply, but I think I need some more time to sort myself out completely.

I don't want to agree to this just because I don't want to disappoint her or because I feel envious of my married colleagues. I need to be really convinced that I want this because I believe in it fully. I am not unsure of Helen, nor do I want to be with anyone else other than her. I think then it is just a matter of spending some time in Contemplation about this matter to find clarity. From today, I will find some time every evening to Adioscope this for a few minutes each day so I can find the right answer.

CHAPTER TAKEAWAYS:

- Focusing too much on the outside can leave you disconnected from the inside.
- Relying on external praise, appreciation, attention may feel good in the moment but might leave you restless in the long run.

- Living your life looking inward rather than outward helps you understand yourself better, your interests, strengths and what makes you more peaceful.
- A strong inner connection ensures that you don't get tempted by distractions in the external environment to make a wrong decision. If you look inward regularly, you make decisions that are right for your peace of mind.
- Looking inward allows you to discover, appreciate and live your own story rather than trying to live someone else's.

17. PRINCIPLE TWELVE: FORM VS SUBSTANCE

In a world that often emphasizes appearances, external achievements, and superficial measures of success, adopting the principle of substance over form allows us to make choices that align with what makes us feel fulfilled, purposeful, and peaceful.

Form simply means the outer appearance of something while substance refers to the essence and inherent value that underlie a certain appearance or form. When you live your life focusing on substance, you align your choices with your core values, inner peace, and long-term well-being. When you focus on substance, you pay attention to the underlying qualities, intentions, and impact of your actions. You pay attention to what really matters.

Appearance vs Substance - this is a question that can arise in many situations. It may arise in work, in a relationship or various roles such as a parent, leader, etc. that you might play in your life. In each instance, you need to be able to clearly distinguish between the form and the substance in that situation and focus on what brings you more fulfillment and peace of mind.

Form could be how classy an office looks, how pretty a website is, or how famous an organization is. Substance could be the purpose of that office, how useful the website is, what the organization actually does, what it stands for and its net impact on people's well-being.

Form could be the impressive speeches a leader delivers, the promises they make and the image they create in the eyes of the public, while substance could be their true character, whether they keep their promises and whether they really care for their audience even when they are not looking.

Form could be the state-of-the-art facilities of an expensive school your kids attend, while substance could be the quality of education they receive, the personality and character of the teachers and the overall philosophy of the school to prepare your child for a fulfilling and peaceful life. The softer aspects of a school matter a lot more and can stay with the students for life.

What areas of your life can you think of where you can clearly differentiate between appearance and substance? Do you tend to focus too much on appearance and ignore the substance?

Sarah had always dreamed of working in a glamorous industry, surrounded by sleek offices, high-profile clients, and a constant buzz of excitement. She landed a job at a prestigious advertising agency, where the exterior appearance of success was carefully cultivated. The office space was modern and stylish, the company had a strong reputation, and her colleagues seemed to exude confidence and sophistication.

Initially, Sarah felt a sense of pride and satisfaction from being a part of such an organization. She loved her fancy job title and the glamorous events she attended. However, as time went on, Sarah began to realize that the form—the superficial aspects of her workplace—was overshadowing the substance—the true purpose and fulfillment she sought from her work.

She found herself caught up in the whirlwind of presentations, meetings, and networking events, always striving to maintain a polished image and meet external expectations. Sarah realized that this emphasis on appearances was detracting from the meaningful work she wanted to do. She was forcing a smile even when she was miserable on the inside. The creative projects she had initially been excited about took a backseat to the pressure of meeting clients' demands and chasing after recognition.

As Sarah reflected on her experience, she came to understand that the true substance of her work lay in the ability to do something meaningful, bring innovative ideas to life, and connect with people on a deeper level. Her peace of mind depended on the quality of work she had produced during the month and not the number of celebrity events she had attended. She realized that although she was smitten by it earlier, the external glamor and prestige of her workplace were superficial in nature and didn't provide the fulfillment she was really looking for. It was killing her soul bit by bit. She was feeling suffocated.

Sarah decided to redefine her career path. She sought out opportunities that aligned with her values and allowed her to utilize her creativity to make a difference. She transitioned to a purpose-driven organization working on climate tech, where she could have a more direct impact and work with like-minded individuals who shared her vision. The company parties were simpler, but genuine, without anyone trying to put up false appearances or flashing designer dresses and expensive handbags.

She realized that while the allure of external appearances can be tempting, it is the substance—the core purpose and meaning—of her work that ultimately brought her a deep sense of satisfaction and peace of mind.

Does your work provide you with a sense of meaning and purpose today? If you close your eyes and think about it, does it make you feel fulfilled and peaceful? Do you feel energized to do your best?

John had recently completed his MBA degree and was faced with the decision of what career path to pursue. He was drawn to the prestige and allure of management consulting—a field known for its high-profile clients, challenging projects, and impressive salaries and perks. The form of the profession, with its glamorous reputation and opportunities for rapid career advancement, seemed irresistible to John.

Driven by the external perceptions and societal expectations associated with management consulting, John decided to join a renowned consulting firm. He was quickly swept up in the fast-paced and demanding nature of the job. His days were filled with client meetings, data analysis, and producing reports to meet tight deadlines. On the surface, everything seemed perfect.

However, as time went on, John began to feel a sense of restlessness and dissatisfaction. He realized that despite the external manifestations of success, the substance of his work—the true purpose and fulfillment he sought—was lacking. Deep down, John had always been passionate about getting his own hands dirty. He loved manufacturing and had a deep understanding of its inner workings growing up. He had a natural talent for optimizing production processes and really getting into the grind to improve efficiency.

While he had learned a lot in his consulting work over the past few years, he hadn't really taken any real responsibility to make a client successful in the true sense. Often, the recommendations they made to the client were very intellectual and theoretical in nature that reminded him of his case study class back in school. While they churned out fancy reports that talked about how the future would look, they were really extrapolating the past rather than creating something new for the future. He wanted to create something himself.

As John reflected on his career choice, he acknowledged that he had been swayed by the form—the external image and perceived prestige of management consulting, and of course the money that it had to offer. It was just too hard to resist. He realized that he had neglected the substance—the true essence of who he was and what he was meant to do. The glamor of consulting couldn't replace the joy and fulfillment he experienced when working on the shop floor.

John finally found the courage to leave his consulting job behind and pursue his dream of running a manufacturing company. He accepted the challenges and uncertainties that came with this new path, knowing that it would bring him closer to his authentic self.

It wasn't all roses for the first few years, but he eventually found himself thriving in his work and felt much more fulfilled and peaceful. The greasy clothes made him feel joy that his neatly ironed designer suits had never known. His work had meaning and purpose. It reflected who he really was deep down.

He used his expertise and passion to streamline operations and optimize supply chains. He trained his team in Contemplation so they could create innovation at will and together they went on to redefine established industry norms that had been taken for granted for many years. He declared an official Contemplation Hour every Tuesday as a ritual built into the company culture, where all employees could take an hour to think about the Adios principles so they could reduce their personal and work stress, think more deeply to find new insights, and connect better with the values and mission of the organization. That led to fewer sick days off, lower mental health doctor costs, higher intrinsic motivation and productivity and innovation delivered systematically every quarter.

He certainly used some of his knowledge from his consulting days, but he had now found where he belonged. Although the appearance of his previous career choice seemed glamorous, it couldn't compare to the fulfillment and sense of purpose he experienced in his new role. He also understood that had he not experienced the consulting world for a few years, he might not have appreciated this life as much as he did today.

Sometimes the illusion of form can distract you from your true calling. You must make time for Contemplation so you can know yourself better, because only you can do that. By prioritizing the substance—the core essence of who you are and what brings you fulfillment, you can make career choices that align with your authentic self and create a lasting sense of peace and happiness.

It is ideal if you can choose your work thoughtfully early in your career. But even if you were not able to do that, it is not too late. Think about what will really make you feel fulfilled and peaceful in the long run and make the right decision today. If as a leader you feel that under the pressure of external expectations, you stopped listening to the right voice inside of you and started making decisions that you feel are not right, go for a Contemplation walk today. Find that voice. Repeat it in your mind. Say it aloud if necessary. Contemplation not only helps you find clarity. If you stay with that clarity long enough, it also gives you the courage to act on that clarity. Try it for a few days.

Appearance vs Substance can also be relevant in your relationships.

Emily had been dating Mark for a few months, and their relationship seemed to be progressing well. Mark had a charming and charismatic personality, always bringing thoughtful gifts and saying all the right things. They watched movies and went on vacation together. On the surface, it appeared as though their relationship was flourishing, with all the elements of a romantic connection.

However, as time went on, Emily started to feel a growing disconnect between them. While Mark's gestures and polite words were nice to have, she realized that they didn't necessarily reflect the true essence of their connection. What truly mattered to Emily was shared values, genuine care for each other and emotional intimacy.

Emily longed for deeper conversations where they could explore their dreams, fears, and vulnerabilities. She desired a partner who could provide emotional support and truly understand her on a profound level. She needed a relationship where they could laugh together, but also be comfortable staying silent as they lay next to each other. Most importantly, she wanted someone who could also understand her spiritual journey because it was an important part of her existence. While Mark was polite and help- ful, was that enough? Even though she had nothing really to complain about Mark, she wasn't thriving with him.

Recognizing this misalignment, Emily spoke to Mark about how she felt, especially the importance of emotional connection and her spiritual journey. Mark, initially taken aback, realized that he had been focusing more on external appearances rather than nurturing a deeper emotional bond with her. He also realized he was doing so because he was imitating a couple of his colleagues at work who had created a certain display of their personal rela- tionships. In the process, he had forgotten who he truly was and was trying to be someone he wasn't.

Together, they decided to focus on the substance of their relation- ship. They committed to building a genuine connection through deeper and longer conversations, moments of silence together and sharing experiences they both enjoyed. Mark hadn't explored his spiritual side yet, but he said he was open to doing that.

By shifting their focus from the appearance of their relationship to its substance, Emily and Mark discovered a deeper level of understanding, intimacy, and fulfillment in their relationship. They were lucky it was always there somewhere deep inside, but had been lost on the way. They got it back. Many couples don't.

It might be instinctive to focus on appearance because you can see it. Appearance is visible, while substance can be subtle, invisible. But substance is deeper than appearance. Being aware of and focusing on substance can bring you long-term joy, fulfillment, and inner peace. It doesn't mean that appearance should be ignored. It just means that substance should not be ignored.

In which dimensions of your life today can you apply the ADIOS principle of Form vs Substance?

_____

_____

_____

~

PART THREE: ESSAYS

18. CONTEMPLATION, MEDITATION AND MINDFULNESS

MEDITATION IS A POWERFUL PRACTICE. But for it to succeed in the true sense, there are certain pre-conditions. If you don't get them right, your experience and benefits will stay on the surface. You may get glimpses of calmness, clarity, or peace, but you will miss the depth.

It is common to hear from people that meditation isn't working for them. There could be many reasons for this. Here is one of the reasons why Meditation may not be working for you. Think about this for a minute.

You wake up and meditate for a few minutes. You feel relaxed and peaceful at that time.

But if the rest of your day is filled with one or more of these (mentally check what applies to you):

- Criticizing others

- Proving yourself right

- Proving others wrong

- Negatively comparing yourself with others

- Putting others down

- Trying to control others

- Yelling at your colleagues

- Yelling at your family members

- Speaking too much

- Speaking too fast

- Throwing up your hands in disgust

- Rolling your eyes on others

- Blaming others

- Being dependent on external attention, validation, or appreciation

If this is how most of your day looks like, do you think those few minutes of Meditation in the morning will work for you?

You first need to remove the noise from your system. Clear the noise so Meditation can happen.

The Adios system helps you remove that noise. When you use Contemplation to think through the Adios principles, you slowly start to remove elements from your life that make you less peaceful and add elements to your life that make you more peaceful. This reduces your overall restlessness. This enables Mediation to happen.

Go to Meditation through Contemplation.

Contemplation and Meditation are complementary. You should do both.

You work on removing the noise elements mentioned above using Contemplation. You become aware of them, think deeply about them, study their negative impact on your peace of mind, and eliminate them from your daily routine, slowly, step by step. You also add positive elements to your life.

As you start to do that, you find a clearer You, a calmer You, a more peaceful You. Now this You is ready for Meditation.

Think of Contemplation and Meditation as cousins. You spend your mental energy thinking deeply - in Contemplation. You regain your mental energy through Meditation.

Recharge your batteries using Meditation. Spend that energy in Contemplation to make the right decisions so you live a peaceful life. Come back and recharge yourself using Meditation. Repeat.

Go to Meditation through Contemplation. That's the right sequence. You can do both at the same time if you want but understand the significance of each practice.

1. Remove the noise using Contemplation and the Adios principles.

2. That prepares your body and mind for calmness, deep thought and focus.

3. Go to Meditation.

Meditation is a powerful tool, but only if you know how to use it well.

It can seem too abstract sometimes. It seems abstract because it is. But there is a particular way to go about it.

You don't go to the abstract directly. You go gradually via the real.

You don't go to the subconscious directly. You go gradually via the conscious.

You don't go to the subtle directly. You go gradually via the gross.

You don't go to Mediation directly. You go gradually via Contemplation.

From the real to the abstract.

From the conscious to the subconscious.

From the gross to the subtle.

From Contemplation to Meditation.

Contemplation provides the context to Meditation. If Meditation hasn't worked for you, it might work well if you go through Contemplation. If Meditation has already brought benefits to you, adding Contemplation will help you go deeper into your Meditation practice.

Contemplation prepares your body to be calm, so your meditation can go deeper.

Contemplation prepares your mind to be peaceful, so your meditation can go deeper.

Contemplation prepares you to look within, so your meditation can go deeper.

Meditation is the lock. Contemplation is the key. You aren't using the key but are wondering why the lock isn't opening.

Think about it this way. You want to have cold water (a peaceful life), but currently you have boiling water with you (a restless life as described above). Because you want quick relief, a silver bullet, you jump to Meditation directly without going through the preparatory process of Contemplation. That is like trying to add a couple of ice cubes to the boiling water to create instant cold water. It won't work. You may find pockets of clarity of peace here and there, but the overall water will remain hot, your overall life will remain restless.

Contemplation helps you go through the process systematically - first turn off the flame (get away from elements in your life that keep you boiling / restless), then let the water cool down slowly (practice the Adios principles to remove the restlessness slowly and steadily), and once the water is cool enough, add ice to it (with a calmer body and mind, go into deeper states of Meditation).

The Patanjali Yoga Sutras define an 8-step process to achieve the highest state of consciousness:

1. Yamas - Don'ts (to reduce restlessness)
2. Niyamas - Do's (to reduce restlessness)
3. Asana - Physical stillness
4. Pranayama - Systematic breathing
5. Pratyahara - Withdrawing the senses within
6. Dharana - Concentration
7. Dhyana - Meditation
8. Samadhi - Highest state of consciousness / union

The way this system works is - if you 'do' the first five, the remaining three 'happen'. Each of the first five steps exist so you systematically remove restlessness from your system, so that you go into deeper states of meditation.

If you work on incorporating the Yamas and Niyamas into your daily life, you start to become less restless. If you practice physical stillness, you become less restless. If you practice slow breathing, you become less restless. If you withdraw your senses from the external world, you become less restless. When you have 'done' all of this, you have become a significantly less restless person. Then, Meditation 'happens' much more easily.

The problem today is that you don't work on the Yamas and Niyamas, physical stillness or withdrawing the senses, but you directly jump to step Seven. You want to 'do' Meditation. The water is still boiling. You want to put a couple of ice cubes into it to get instant cold water.

If you have been living a very restless, outward focused, fast-paced life, and if you start to practice a few minutes of Medita-tion where you sit quietly, just those few moments of silence can sometimes be very profound because of the stark contrast it bears to your current restless and noisy life. So, you feel a notice-able change. And yes, that might be a real change you are experi-encing. But you might mistake the trailer for the movie. You might start to celebrate the two-minute trailer without realizing that the whole movie is ninety minutes long. There is a lot more that is possible. You have just tasted a few water molecules that were very close to those ice cubes, so they felt cool. But you continue to live a restless life during the day, thinking that 'doing' Meditation in the morning covers it all. It doesn't.

It isn't about 'doing' Meditation for few minutes each day. It is about staying meditative throughout the day - every hour, every minute. Meditation isn't like working out at the gym for a few minutes and you are done for the day. It is like your diet plan. You don't just eat healthy stuff for 45 mins in the morning and forget all about it during the day. You need to eat healthy throughout the day. Given the restless nature of the fast-paced world today, Meditation is being considered as a one-time work-out, a morning to-do item that you can check off. It doesn't work like that. It never will. Staying Meditative. Not doing Medita-tion. 'ive', not 'ion'. That's the key. It is a state, not an activity. A state to stay in, not an activity to be checked off.

How does your day look like today? How do you feel? Peaceful, contemplative, meditative throughout the day? You speak very less, speak very slowly, don't use negative speech - no anger, criticism, sarcasm, you don't compare yourself with others negatively and feel inferior, don't seek external appreciation or attention, always choose the voice that makes you more peaceful, don't experience an urge to prove anything to anyone, don't have an impatience to share things instantly, don't do or say things just because they feel good in the moment but are not right for you, share a deeply caring and loving relationship with your partner, your kids, your siblings, your parents, your work is like your mission that brings meaning and purpose in your life and not just money?

Or do you feel restless?

Go to Meditation through Contemplation. Go deeper into Meditation using Contemplation.

If there are fifty people shaking a car and one of them stops but the remaining 49 continue to shake it, will the car stop shaking? If there are fifty parts vibrating in a machine and one of them stops but the remaining 49 continue to vibrate, will the machine stop vibrating?

If there are 50,000 people shouting at a stadium and 1,000 of those stop but the remaining 49,000 continue to shout, will the stadium go quiet? If there are 50,000 firecrackers going off in the sky and 1,000 of them stop but the remaining 49,000 keep exploding, will the sky go quiet?

If you are active for 50,000 seconds (~ 14 hours) in a day but you are still and peaceful only for 1,000 seconds (~15 mins) a day during your meditation session while being restless for the remaining 49,000 seconds, will your day be peaceful? If you continue to do this for 80 years every day, will your life be peaceful?

Those 1000 seconds of stillness and peace is a good start, but remember you have another 49,000 seconds to master. Go from

1,000 to 2,000, then 5,000, then 10,000 seconds. Go from meditation to meditative.

How far do you want to go? That is your choice. Only practicing Contemplation on the Adios principles can enable you to live a fulfilling, purposeful and peaceful life. If you wish to go deeper, use Meditation.

The urge to speak and connect with others is built into our behavour. That is a good tool to make connections in the outside world. There are people in the outside world and the best way to connect with them and get to know them is by speaking with them. Similarly, if you wish to make your connection with your inside world, you need to stop speaking to the people outside and focus on the person within.

Sometimes when you start your inward journey, you might continue to use your existing tools and behaviors you use in the outside world. Because you are so used to them, it feels natural to apply them in this process as well. Your habit of being chatty might come from external world experience, but if you continue that chattiness during your inward journey, it will be detrimental to your progress.

You might experience some change, lightness, joy, etc. but your practice will never go very deep. In the outside world, you are used to socializing in groups and communities to share thoughts, opinions and experiences. So, you might tend to apply the same habit to your inward journey. You might join meditation or mindfulness communities to go down that path, but your real inner driving force might continue to remain making more social connections externally, rather than creating a deeper connection internally. You might be restless about what others think, how their experience was, impatiently share your experience with others, and continue to react in an animated manner to others' opinions and experiences, just like you would at a social event.

When you do this, you are simply continuing to use your tools and behaviors from the external world. Your key purpose continues to be chatting with others, feeling more socially connected with others or even making new friends. It is natural to feel that connecting to like-minded individuals in a field is helpful, because that is what you have seen in your experience with the outside world, so you use the same methods for your inward journey. You connected with others for parties, camping, dining. Now you connect with others for meditation. But the need to connect with others remains. You chatted with others about movies, family, and entertainment. Now you chat about your and others' meditation experience. But the urge to chat remains. The restlessness remains.

So does this mean you have made no progress at all? What about that lightness or calmness that you have been feeling? Does it mean you have been wasting your time? Not necessarily. What it means is that you have begun your journey and are on your way, but you can get better and go deeper, and to do that, a lot more can be done.

But just because a lot more can be done doesn't mean you must do it. The question is - do you want to do it? You need to decide that. It is your life. Do you wish to be an amateur seeker? Do you wish to be a hobbyist seeker? Or do you want to go deeper? You don't have to. It is your choice. But you need to be clear.

It is similar to any other discipline in the external world. Thousands of people study physics, but most don't go deep enough to become an Einstein or Newton. Thousands of people study the piano, but most don't go deep enough to become a Beethoven. Thousands of people play basketball, but most don't go deep enough to become a Michael Jordan.

So as an amateur or a hobbyist musician, you might get together with friends, play some music together, chat and have fun. You can get together with friends to play basketball over the weekend and have fun. Nothing wrong with that. But if you wish to go deeper, then casual practice doesn't work. If you want to be a pro, you need to practice like a pro. Pros don't practice like amateurs or hobbyists. They practice like pros. So, you need to be clear. Do you wish to be an amateur or a hobbyist seeker? Or do you wish to go deeper.

You don't need that clarity from the very beginning. You could start as an amateur and somewhere along the way find a desire to go deeper. It is a process that works differently for different people. You need to find your specific path. But don't apply the rules of mastering the external world to mastering the internal world.

If you do this, you might miss the point completely. You might miss the opportunity completely. You may begin to use words such as divine, heal, connect with the universe, consciousness, because those words subconsciously make you feel that you have arrived but on the inside you might remain restless. You may not embody any stillness or peace in your own self.

The restlessness hasn't gone away in that case. It is still present in each cell of your body. The desire for instant gratification still remains. The desire to speak a lot remains. Silence hasn't become your best friend yet. Your mind isn't cleansed yet. There is much work yet to be done to still the body, still the mind, remove rest-lessness from the body and mind. You have experienced some-thing, and that something is probably real - the lightness, the calmness - but it hasn't yet seeped into every cell of your body. The remaining 49,000 people in your stadium are still shouting. So that calmness is short-lived. But you might take that as the ultimate. You might take that as the destination and conclude the journey has ended, when in fact it has just begun.

This is the path of an amateur, a hobbyist. Enjoy playing music with amateurs, make new friends, chat and have a good time. Enjoy playing ball with amateurs, make new friends, chat and have a good time. Enjoy meditation with amateurs, make new friends, chat and have a good time.

Meditation and Meditainment are not the same. Know the difference.

In such instances, you might also have a pro musician or ball player or an experienced meditation teacher with you, but the motions might remain the same. You might notice a stark difference between the mannerisms of the experienced teacher and those of the others, but only if you know what to look for. If you are too busy soaking in the excitement and fun, nodding your head vigorously to the experiences shared by others because you want to feel like a community - involved and concerned - you will miss creating a connection with yourself because you are busy connecting with the external world. The focus remains on the outside world, not on the inside world. Your mind is not always your friend, so you need to be careful, watchful, cautious. Contemplation helps you do that.

The Adios system is built as a mental cleansing program (chitta shuddhi kriya) and is in a sense an implementation program for the Yama, Niyama, Asana, Pratyahara and Dharana sections of the Patanjali Yoga Sutras. Once you 'do the work' on these, Dhyana (Meditation) happens, and deepens.

This will also help you systematically awaken your Kundalini energy. But even if it awakens, if you haven't done the fundamental cleansing work to reduce the restlessness using Contemplation and the Adios principles, the energy will have very little impact in your life, and you will end up wasting its potential.

The purpose of the Kundalini is to enable you to experience higher states of consciousness, which is not possible if you haven't done the cleansing work. Why? Because consciousness means awareness. Awareness means paying attention. So, a high state of consciousness means the ability to create a constant stream of attention on your inner world. If you have restlessness in your system, it won't allow you to reach those mental states, because there is too much other noise that is disturbing you.

Your Kundalini will be effective only to the extent of the work you have done within. Think of it this way. You don't have water in your city. Someone from another city offers to connect their water pipe to your city's water pipe and supply you the water. But if your own water pipe is clogged with dirt, no matter how much water is coming in from the other side, you won't be able to use it because there is too much noise in your pipe.

Unless you do the work, you won't get deeper results. Don't look for silver bullets or short cuts. They don't exist. Yes, it feels good to look for a short cut, but does it feel right?

Go to Meditation through Contemplation. Use the Adios principles to cleanse your system, and use Meditation to deepen the experience of your life.

Contemplation and Mindfulness

While mindfulness emphasizes being present in the moment, Contemplation goes a step further by guiding you to make conscious choices that lead to inner peace. Think of Adios as a systematic, practical and granular system to implement mindfulness. Using Adios, you are being mindful about your inner voices, about your choices, about your speech, about what makes you more fulfilled and peaceful, about what feels good but doesn't feel right, about whether you are too focused on external validation, appreciation or attention, etc. Look at the Adios principles as detailed mindfulness markers that you can apply to your personal and professional life.

While mindfulness emphasizes non-judgmental awareness of the present moment, Contemplation directs your attention to the process of decision-making and provides you with a framework - the Adios principles - to help you make the right decisions. It also provides you with your personal decision-making tool - Adioscope - that helps you make the right personal or professional decisions. It doesn't tell you what to do. It empowers you to find the answer that is right for you. Only you can find it.

Contemplation provides you a step-by-step method to reduce the restlessness prevalent in today's fast-paced life.

The Adios framework is in essence a mindfulness framework, a very detailed, practical and systematic mindfulness framework. The practice of Contemplation on the Adios principles helps you stay mindful of what you do, say or think as you go through your day. The Adioscope provides you with a decision-making tool so you can make decisions that are right for you - should I quit my job, should we buy this house, should our kids go to this school, should I start my own business, should we move to that city, etc.

Use the habit of Contemplation to stay mindful throughout the day. Use the Adios principles to create your own decision-making system. Use the Adioscope to make decisions that are right for you. When you make the right decisions, that leads to a more fulfilling, purposeful, and peaceful life.

It's not difficult. Even if you made some bad decisions in the past, forget what you did until yesterday. Start today and your tomorrow will change. The world around you may still be the same, but your ability to deal with that world, your ability to remain calm amidst chaos will be significantly better.

19. MEASURING MENTAL FITNESS USING THE ONENESS QUOTIENT (OQ)

MOST PEOPLE TODAY live their life largely looking outward and not inward, so they are not deeply connected with themselves, so they lack internal clarity, so they tend to make choices that seem exciting in the short run but are not right for them in the long run. That causes most of modern stress today.

Most people are not unwell. They are unclear.

Most people don't need therapy. They need clarity.

A few of those might need clinical intervention if they have crossed a certain risk or behavior threshold. But most others are unclear, not unwell.

The Adios approach is if you train your inner counselor, you will never need to depend on an external one.

If you don't have clarity within, no therapist can really help you. Unless you do the work on your own, internally, you won't find that clarity. Therapy can sometimes also become a lazy option where you hope that someone else can solve my problems or give me a silver bullet and all will be well. It doesn't work that way. You need to do the work. Your well-being is your responsibility, not someone else's.

While some people might benefit from therapy or medicines, many of those benefits may last only for a short while if sufficient work on the fundamental internal clarity hasn't been done. It is like going for a vacation or to a party to take your mind off the problem for some time. You can avoid it or distract yourself temporarily. But that may not solve the root of the problem - your lack of clarity. Your therapist might have worked hard to help you. But you need to put in the work.

If you lack clarity, you may choose the wrong partner, or say / do wrong things to your partner, choose a wrong job, choose a wrong liquid or substance, make your happiness too dependent on external attention or appreciation, etc. That adds up and creates stress and anxiety. Taken to an extreme, it becomes dangerous and might need a mental health doctor.

Also, mental health has been defined very narrowly today. The phrase mental health today means mental illness - anxiety, depression etc. But just because you are not mentally ill doesn't mean you are mentally well.

If you are restless

If you rush to prove yourself right and others wrong

If you constantly put others down in a discussion

If you negatively compare yourself with others and feel inferior

If you do things that feel good in the moment but aren't right for you in the long run

If you can't understand multiple voices in your head and choose the one that makes you more peaceful

If you speak too much

If you speak too fast

If you focus too much on external validation, attention, or appreciation.

In all of these cases, you may not suffer from depression or anxiety, so you may not be mentally ill, but you are also not mentally well. You are not mentally thriving. The Adios principles address these aspects of your personality, so you solve the root of the problem, rather than only soothe the symptoms temporarily.

Traditional therapy is meant to solve illnesses that show certain symptoms. But as I mentioned earlier, most people aren't unwell. They are unclear.

We need to train the therapists and counselors in the Adios system as well so they can incorporate it into their medical knowledge and offer an integrated solution to the problem. This will make their therapy much stronger because it will be a combination of external and self-therapy. This is guaranteed to show drastic improvement in the mental health of the people who seek such therapy.

The patients and their families will be grateful to their therapists for teaching them how to find their own solutions and maintain a clear and peaceful mind on an ongoing basis. The therapists will feel more fulfilled and peaceful because they work hard to help their patients get well and this integrated approach will make more patients well, and for a long time.

The gamut of mental health needs to be expanded beyond illnesses such as anxiety, depression, etc. and include situations where people may not be mentally ill but are also not mentally well. That's the majority of the people in the world today. The mental health problem, in a sense, is far far larger than the mental illness problem. The mental illness problem is, in some cases, the mental fitness problem taken to a dangerous extreme.

The therapist/psychiatrist can start with a combination of medical treatments and Adios with the objective of eventually helping them wean away from the medicines and run their life only on Adios as their mental fitness system. This is the integrated Mind + Molecule approach to mental health. Some people might need the molecule if their condition is severe, but once they feel better, the mind approach needs to take over to help them run the remaining part of their life in an efficient manner. Traditional therapy and Adios are complementary. They work great together as a team.

Listening to nature sounds or soothing music before going to bed might relax or entertain you at the moment, but it also doesn't solve the problem at a fundamental level. You are the same person in the morning that you were the night before. The root of the problem remains. But you are older by a few hours. And these hours soon turn into days, and days turn into months, and months turn into years. If you aren't careful, you will leave this world without really knowing yourself well, and without understanding why you don't feel fulfilled and peaceful even though you seem to have many of the success markers the world considers to be important.

Most people leave this world without knowing themselves well. Please don't be that person.

Mental fitness can be measured using the Oneness Quotient (OQ). Your OQ tells you what percent of the time you make such decisions that make you more peaceful. It is a measure of how well you are connected with yourself, how well you know what makes you feel fulfilled, purposeful and peaceful. It is a measure of your intrapersonal intelligence.

There are two components to maintaining a high OQ:

- Having a deep connection with yourself

- Having a personal decision-making system that helps you make the right choices

A deep connection with yourself created using a habit of Contemplation will help you understand what makes you feel fulfilled and peaceful. Your personal decision-making system (Adioscope) will help you make such choices that make you feel fulfilled and peaceful.

The parameters of OQ are the elements we have discussed in this book in the chapters containing the Adios principles - how well can you understand your multiple voices, how capable are you in choosing the right voice in a given situation, how well can you control your urge to prove or negatively compare yourself with others, how well can you manage the quantity and velocity of your speech, etc. You can check your OQ by taking the OQ assessment for free on www.adiosworld.com.

OQ is not only an individual level metric. You can have a team OQ, a departmental OQ, an organizational OQ, a city OQ, a state OQ and a country OQ.

A high OQ organization would mean a highly aligned workforce that can use Contemplation to maximize their own as well as the organizational potential, find innovation and creativity in a systematic manner, have strong team bonding and sense of purpose and alignment, make decisions faster, make fewer wrong decisions, fail fast but fail smartly and only if really necessary (rather than wearing the fail fast badge as a badge of honor), and all this with lower stress hence a much smaller employee mental health bill to pay.

A high OQ city or state will mean citizens who feel more fulfilled, purposeful, and peaceful. They love and respect each other more. They stress less. They contribute to their communities joyfully. They welcome others with a smile. Less anger, aggression or violence. More camaraderie and contentment. A city or state isn't smart merely because of technology. It is really smart when the members live a fulfilling life. What would you rather have - a high-tech state but with stressed and miserable people or one where people feel fulfilled and joyful?

A high OQ education institution means students who are clearer about what they want to do and why, so they don't choose wrong careers. Students who are deep thinkers hence can think of solutions that don't exist today. A high OQ biotech organization would mean having the power of Contemplation to speed up the discovery of the next molecule.

The possibilities are endless.

If you make decisions based on short-term satisfaction, that might lead to lack of peace, so you might resort to short-term solutions such as therapy or liquids or pills which don't solve the root of the problem but just postpone the misery by a few hours, until you make another decision for short-term satisfaction. And the cycle continues.

To create a high OQ world, we need two things:

- A deep connection with oneself
- A personal decision-making system that helps us make the right decisions.

Contemplation helps you create and maintain a deep connection with yourself. The Adios principles help you create a personal decision-making system that helps you make such decisions that lead to a fulfilled, purposeful, and peaceful life.

Train your inner counselor, so you never need to depend on an external one. Only you know what is right for you, what makes you feel fulfilled and peaceful. No one else does.

Think about it.

20. ADIOS FOR WORK: WHAT IS A SUCCESSFUL ORGANIZATION?

OUR GOAL IS to build a successful organization, but before we do that, we must clearly define the term "success". If you define success to only mean financial success, or building a large organization, or a market leader, or growing as quickly as possible, etc., then your mind will get to work to achieve that goal for you and your actions will be determined by only that goal. However, if you were to define the goal differently, if you define the problem statement differently, then the same mind will now get to work to achieve this new objective.

For example, if you define the objective as - I want to find a drug that cures fever, you might find a drug that cures fever but after that it leaves the person in a coma. If, however, you define the problem statement differently and say - I want to find a drug that cures fever and does not have any significant side effects on their life, then your mind will accept that revised objective and look for a solution accordingly. Your mind, remember. Not you. Your mind does everything for you and your body follows. So it is important that you understand how the mind works, its pitfalls, its temptations, and understand ways to improve its effectiveness so that you achieve success that bears a superior quality.

So let us define "success" appropriately. Here is how we will define it. Our overarching goal is not to create a successful organization, or to cure cancer, or to reduce CO_2 or to go to the Moon. Our overarching objective is to create a fulfilling, purposeful and peaceful life. That's our primary objective. Everything else that we do in our life must flow from that. It must be a subset of that.

Let's unpack that - a fulfilling, purposeful and peaceful life. Let's start with the word "life". Life is what happens to us each day, so let us look at the key components of life - the ones where you either spend a lot of your time, or the ones that mean a lot to you.

Life is broadly about work, relationships, parenting, education, self growth, and a few other things that might be important to you. If you visualize this as an equation:

Life = Work + Relationships + Parenting + Education + Self Growth + A Few Other Important Things

So if you are aiming for a fulfilling, purposeful and peaceful life, which is the left hand side of this equation, you won't have it unless the components on the right hand side of the equation are also fulfilling, purposeful and peaceful. So unless your work, relationships, parenting, education, self growth etc. are also fulfilling, purposeful and peaceful, your life won't be.

If you are working full time, then you might spend a large number of your waking hours working or thinking about work even if you are not working actively. Hence, if your work is not fulfilling, if it doesn't bring meaning and purpose in your life, if it is stressful rather than peaceful, your life might feel unfulfilled, meaningless and stressed. Similarly relationships might hold a strong place in your life so unless they are fulfilling and peaceful, your life won't be. Similarly, there could be other things that matter to you in life.

So when you define "success" at work, you must ask - Is my work fulfilling, purposeful and peaceful? If you define it as only financial success, or fame, or achieving certain social parameters of success, you might miss out on certain key elements that might define the quality of your life. You might look good in the eyes of others, but you might not feel complete within. The quality of your life depends on how you feel, so if you feel unfulfilled and stressed, the social success factors may not matter much.

Why achieve only financial success when you can also achieve a fulfilling, purposeful and peaceful work life? The emphasis is on 'also'. You just need to define the objective correctly, so you can focus on the right things.

After the word 'life', now let us look at the word 'peaceful'. By saying we want work to be peaceful, we are not implying that we must be lazy, or complacent or easy-going. We just mean that it should not carry unnecessary stress or anxiety or restlessness on a regular basis. We might work really hard, long hours if we want to, but it should not be accompanied by stress and anxiety. Your relationships don't have to fall apart because of your work. Your ability to become a role model for your child should not be compromised because of your work. Your ability to take care of your loved ones should not be impacted because of your work.

Why are we worried about all this? Because setting the wrong priorities and defining success only as achieving financial or social success as fast as possible almost always leads to these problems, which then means that your life does not eventually turn out to be fulfilling, purposeful and peaceful. Such problems can also arise if you immerse yourself in an illusion that your work is extremely important and really urgent so you must compromise on everything else. Because the world is ending, you tell yourself, I must make these personal sacrifices. It is almost always never true, unless it is a really short-term emergency like a building on fire or the hospital emergency room.

Huge, really huge long term problems can be solved at least ten times more efficiently if you work on them without an unnecessary sense of urgency or restlessness. Some of those problems might have been created due to the restlessness of some individuals in the first place. Don't fight fire with fire. So work being peaceful means work without unnecessary stress, anxiety or restlessness. That gives you the ability to make the right decisions, rather than making decisions that might feel exciting in the short run but do not lead to a fulfilled, purposeful and peaceful world in the long run.

The word 'fulfilling' covers financial success as an objective. It also covers maximizing your potential, intellectual fulfillment, etc. But work that is only fulfilling without being peaceful can sometimes be dangerous. If you have a restless mind that is given to short-term gratification or pursuing goals that sound exciting but may not have a healthy outcome, fulfillment of such a restless mind might not necessarily be a positive thing. A mob might feel fulfilled after lynching someone. A sales professional might feel fulfilled after selling a wrong product to someone, only because it meets their target. A product manager might feel fulfilled after creating a product that is exciting. But if the outcome is detrimental to the quality of life of others, then such fulfillment is misguided.

In some cases, you might be well intentioned but just ignorant of what is really right or wrong. Short term excitement or peer pressure or current trends or an aggressive leader can often blind you to the long term consequences of your actions. Take your time. Use your Adioscope to think through such critical decisions in life. Don't rush into them. Have a dialogue in silence with yourself. Frequently.

'Purposeful' in the context of an organization means that it has a strong Non Financial Vision that inspires everyone. We will talk more about that later on.

Recall that we are building an organization that is not only fulfilling, purposeful and peaceful but also financially successful. To build an organization like this, you can use the Adios Organizational Framework.

The five layers of this framework starting from the bottom to the top are Values, Non Financial Vision, Culture, Objectives and Key Results (OKRs) and Compensation. Here is how you stack them:

5. Compensation

4. OKRs

3. Culture

2. Non Financial Vision

1. Values

You start with the first layer - Values. You ask - what are the key guiding principles that we will never compromise on as an organization? What do we stand for no matter what? What will we continue to stand for even if we were to lose revenue to stay true to it? The Values of an organization could be a combination of the values of the team members and in addition, certain values that apply specifically to the organization because of its nature of service (e.g. data privacy of its customers, mental wellbeing of its users, etc.).

The next question to ask is - Using these Values, what Non Financial Vision do we wish to achieve as a team? What inspires us?

A Non Financial Vision is defined as a desire to either improve a process or a system, or to improve someone's quality of life. A strong Non Financial Vision can bring together an inspired team, and can keep them inspired for a long time, especially when the chips are down.

The third tier of the Adios Organizational Framework is Culture. So you ask - With these Values, to achieve this Non Financial Vision, what Culture should we have at our organization? What are our people doing on a daily basis? What are they not doing? Culture is behavior repeated on a regular basis. How people conduct themselves on a day to day basis, what they do and don't do, what gets talked about frequently during meetings, how people think on a daily basis becomes the culture.

So in addition to defining the role skill sets and qualifications, you also need to define the behavioral characteristics of the team members. Keep the filter - fulfilling, purposeful and peaceful - in mind as you define them. This creates your Intended Culture. Your Intended Culture document should drive your hiring strategy, not the other way around.

Very often, organizations start with a goal in mind and hire for roles or positions rather than a fit for Values, Non Financial Vision and Culture. This is because many times the leaders themselves haven't spent enough time in Contemplation to think through their Values, Non Financial Vision and Culture. If you aren't clear, and if you think you are clear but your thinking is misguided, you might end up with the wrong people on the team. Define your Intended Culture and let that drive your hiring strategy. Else you might hire the wrong people, and they will define some kind of a Culture, which may or may not be right for the organization.

The next two tiers are OKRs and Compensation, where you are really saying this is how we will stay on track to achieve our

Non Financial Vision and this is how we will compensate our team during our journey.

While this is the five-tier framework you can use to build your organization, that is not where you start. You start with your individual Values, Non Financial Vision and Culture. Start with the organism and then move to the organization, because an organization is essentially a collection of organisms. Unless you have done the work yourself, individually and are clear about these things at a personal level, you cannot successfully implement them at your organization. Your employees just won't connect with you. To understand why we must start with the individual and not the organization, let us look at why we have failed on this front until today so we don't repeat those mistakes.

Not starting with the organism, the individual, has been the primary problem for the last many years when organizations have tried to implement these things. Values, vision, mission etc. are not new concepts. We have talked about them for years now. But the way they have been implemented until now is suboptimal. This is what usually tends to happen.

A few people gather around a conference table for a few days, define a set of values, vision and mission statements and print them out. Designers are hired. Posters are put up. Now that the definition is done, the next step is to get the employees to adopt them. So presentations are made, instructions are given out, to follow those values and work towards that mission. And that is where the problem lies - following certain values or working towards a mission is not an outside to inside process; it is an inside to outside process. An employee needs to first 'feel' within, feel like following those values, feel motivated to work towards that mission. Cold presentations or mechanical instructions from a supervisor cannot create that feeling. In many instances, the supervisors themselves don't feel it deep within. They are just following orders.

That 'feeling' comes from only one activity - Contemplation - deep thinking. Unless an employee himself or herself goes deep within and thinks about their values, what moves them, drives them, what makes them fulfilled, what makes them peaceful, what non financial vision inspires them at a personal level, they can never create a strong emotional connection with the values or the mission of the organization. Why? Because the basic ability to connect deeply itself is missing. Why? Because the world is noisy and distracting, and most people live their life looking outward and not looking inward. So they do not have a deep connection with themselves, so they are not in touch with their own values and vision. That is why - start with the organism, with the individual.

The sequence is simple: Use Contemplation as the tool to enable your employees to create a deep connection with themselves and their own values and vision, so they are better able to connect with the values and vision of the organization.

Now the fear of a few leaders - But what if some of my employees find that they don't connect with what the organization stands for? Then it is in the interest of both the organization and the employee that you part ways respectfully, and quickly, because the relationship is highly suboptimal - it is a lose-lose relationship. You have a disinterested employee who is probably a quiet quitter not contributing to your mission, and the employee is not maximizing their own potential and perhaps deteriorating their quality of life. The employee may not realize this sometimes because of the attractive paycheck, but as we discussed earlier, spending many hours at unfulfilling work is not good for your life.

As a leader, bite the bullet in the short run and let those people go, so you can create a powerful organization in the long run.

Slow down for a few months so you can skyrocket later on. Else you will continue to drag on with unnecessary weight and eventually get frustrated. You will see bodies in the room but their minds are elsewhere. Let the disinterested ones go. Fast. Incentivize them to leave quickly if you can. They don't fit into your puzzle. Let them find their own puzzle, a place where they will believe, and belong.

Go through the Feels Good vs Feels Right Principle as you think through this situation in your organization. Some things may feel bad in the short term but are good for you in the long run. An organization without disinterested people is a lighter, smoother, faster and more efficient organization. Imagine the energy in the room where you know for sure that everyone is in the room because they really believe, because they want to be, and not just because of their paycheck.

How do you find such disinterested people? Through Contemplation. Speak less. Be silent and focus on the energy of your employees. As you listen to them, observe their work, pay attention and then spend some time in silence thinking about what you feel about this person. The world might have you believe that to be successful you need to 'do'. But 'not doing' periodically is one of the most important responsibilities of a leader. As a leader, you are also the Chief Contemplation Officer of the organization. If you don't think deeply, who will?

How do you find clarity in such cases? Through Contemplation. Silence, slowing down periodically, paying attention to your environment and using the Adioscope will enable you to find such disinterested employees. How do you get the courage and conviction to make a hard decision once you have found them? Through Contemplation. When you feel the power of clarity, and the power of your passion for your Non Financial Vision, that will give you the courage to make some hard decisions. Many people can make hard decisions. Very few can make them with a clear mind, peacefully and gracefully.

No matter how large or small your organization is, if as a leader you are convinced this is the right way to go, you must get started. Better late than never. If you don't change anything today, nothing will change tomorrow. Your today is because of what you did yesterday. For tomorrow to be different, you need to do something different than yesterday, today. So get started. As you make some changes, you can build your Intended Culture document, let go of a few people who don't resonate well, hire the right people as per your Intended Culture, and slowly, you will start to steer the ship in the right direction.

As you go through this exercise, you will also find that most people have goodness inside of them. Many of them have been numbed by the distraction and noise in the external world. So while you might find some who may not resonate well and you might have to let them go, you will also find some existing jewels who are now more energized than ever to work towards the mission of the organization. These are the hidden gems you always had in the organization, but they were either not recognized sufficiently because of the old culture or had themselves forgotten about their passion. Overall, you will only gain tremendously through this overhaul. The gain will significantly overshadow the pain. There is nothing to lose.

So to create an organization where the employees are deeply aligned with its values and vision, you start with yourself first as an individual. From the organism to the organization. Then apply the five-tier Adios Organizational Framework to build and maintain it.

~

21. ADIOS FOR WORK: HOW TO CHOOSE YOUR WORK/ORGANIZATION?

As an employee, you might spend a large number of your waking hours working. So it is important that you choose the kind of work that is best for you. It is important that you do not choose something that may appear to be interesting at the moment but is actually not something that you should be working on.

An exceptionally large number of people today are extremely busy doing what they are not meant to do or what they don't like doing. They work for the paycheck at the end of the month. Doing this deteriorates your quality of life.

It is not good for you because you are limiting your potential. It is not good for your family or your kids because you will fail to inspire them. It is not good for your organization because they are trusting you to work with all your presence but you are not at your best, or busy thinking how to avoid work without getting caught.

It is not good for your personal growth because you are not investing yourself in what you believe in and hence probably not making any effort to improve. It is not good for your conscience and self-esteem because doing something you believe is useful creates self-worth and if you are not interested in the work you do, you will feel a certain hollowness inside of you.

It is a lose-lose-lose transaction on all fronts. Absolutely not worth it.

So how do you think about choosing and then carrying out your work as an employee? Here is a framework you could follow if you are looking for a work opportunity, or if you believe you don't feel fulfilled and inspired with your current work, or you like what you do but you want to take it to the next level in terms of how your work makes you feel.

And don't worry if you are already working or have been working for a long time etc. Start to apply this framework now. Now is good. Now is not too late. Now works.

Here is how to think about work.

Your overarching goal is not to work, or earn money or buy an expensive car, or a larger house, or encash stock options, even though that could be your initial motivation. Your overarching goal is to create a fulfilling, purposeful and peaceful life. That's where you start.

And since you might spend a large number of hours a day and hence a large portion of your life working, if your work is unfulfilling or stressful or lacks meaning and purpose, or creates a negative impact on others, your life may not turn out to be fulfilling. You might be able to draw an attractive compensation, make some friends, create a comfortable, or perhaps a luxurious life in terms of your material needs because money can buy those things. But if your work is not aligned with your values and what makes you peaceful, it is unlikely that you will create a fulfilling, purposeful and peaceful life in the long run.

To create a fulfilling and peaceful life, you need to make such choices that help you create that kind of life for yourself. Wrong choices will create a wrong kind of life. To make the right choices, there are two prerequisites:

1. You must be deeply connected with yourself, and

2. You must have your own system of making the right choices, a system or method that is very personal to you, customized for your life specifically.

So what is the problem?

The problem is that the external world is extremely noisy and distracting, so you might be living your life largely looking outward and not looking inward, so may not be not deeply connected with yourself, so you may not have created that personal system of making the right choices with respect to your work, hence you might make choices that seem exciting in the short term but are actually not right for you in the long term. And that is what leads to stress, anxiety or unnecessary rest-lessness.

Those choices could be which city to work in, which organisa-tion to work with, what kind of work to do, how to carry out that work, what strategies to create and execute at work, etc.

So in the context of your work, the first step, the very first step, is not to look for a company that is well known or offers an attrac-tive compensation, or is working on the latest trends or technol-ogy, etc. The first step is to train yourself to be deeply connected with yourself. And you need to master two technologies for that purpose - Silence and Contemplation.

If you are not deeply connected with yourself, if you don't really know who you are, what kind of work truly aligns with your values and vision, what kind of work will feel meaningful, and what kind of place and people you want to work with, it is possible that you might choose to do something that seems exciting or appropriate today, just for now, but is not right for you in the long term. You might do it perhaps because it looks exciting to you or it is a new trend and everyone is talking about it or many of your friends are doing it too. But chances are:

That is not what you are meant to do.

That is not who you are meant to be.

That is not where you are meant to be.

So the first step is to be deeply connected with yourself. When you choose your work after being deeply connected with yourself, in alignment with your values, your personal vision for your life, what truly provides meaning to you and makes you peaceful, then you become the best version of yourself doing that work. That is when work doesn't really feel like work because it is just an extension of who you are as a person. You are not working. You are just being yourself through the day.

But to get to that stage, you first need to know what this thing called 'being yourself' actually means - do you really know this person called 'yourself'?

Think about a simple situation. Think about how two people become good friends. There is a time when they both are strangers. Then they meet for the first time, maybe talk a little, then meet again and talk some more, and then meet again and again and have more conversations. If the frequency aligns well, they become good friends.

Now replace that second person with yourself. How often have you met yourself, had a conversation with yourself? How regularly do you do that? How many days in a week do you spend time with yourself, all alone, in deep thought? For how many years have you been doing that regularly?

If you haven't really found the time to meet yourself, to get to know yourself, chances are you are making your decisions based on excitement, or impulse, or instinct or you are getting influenced by what others are doing.

It starts with getting to know yourself well. Do that, and the rest will follow.

To be able to get to know yourself deeply, you need to master two technologies - Silence and Contemplation.

To choose the right work or organization for yourself, use the following Adios Career Framework. This is a combination of the Ikigai framework and the Adios approach.

The Adios Career Framework

It is best if your work is an intersection of:

1. What you are good at

2. What you enjoy doing

3. What will pay you

4. What the world needs

5. What you find fulfilling, meaningful and peaceful

It is important that the fifth parameter of the framework is met. Your work must be fulfilling, purposeful and peaceful.

Example 1

- I am good at coding

- I enjoy it

- It pays me

- I code to create something useful (or at least nothing harmful)

- but what I find fulfilling, meaningful and peaceful is elderly care services (for which all the four conditions above are also true).

In this scenario, if I choose coding, I may not feel fulfilled in life.

Example 2

- I am good at financial management

- I enjoy it

- A corporate job will pay me well

- The world can benefit from it

- But what will make me fulfilled is teaching finance at a university (even if at a much lower salary)

In this case, a high paying corporate job might bring worldly success, but may not lead to a fulfilling career.

In some cases, if you know what makes you feel fulfilled, purposeful and peaceful, even if you are not very good at it, you can learn and improve, because you have strong motivation to pursue it. If necessary, you may be willing to compromise financially for some time, or for a long time. But the first thing you need is clarity of thought. You get that through Contemplation.

Choose your work carefully. Don't worry about the years that have passed. You still have many years left in you. If you have made wrong choices in the past and feel that you need to make a change to ensure that your future years are fulfilling and peaceful, take the first step today.

. . .

Contemplation Exercise

Here is your Contemplation exercise for choosing the right work or organisation.

• 20 mins of Contemplation everyday. Go for regular Contemplation walks.

• In your Contemplation session, ask yourself:

◦ What are my values? What are the guiding principles in my life that I will never compromise on?

◦ What is the Non-Financial Vision for my life? A NFV is defined as a desire to either improve a process or a system or to improve someone's quality of life.

◦ What kind of work drives me, moves me, matters to me, and is aligned with my personal values and vision? What kind of work will make me thrive, feel more like an extension of me rather than feel like work and make me stressful?

◦ What kind of work will make me feel fulfilled but also peaceful? If I work on creating something that makes our customers less peaceful or makes them more restless or reduces their quality of life, would that be aligned with my values? Would that make me peaceful?

◦ What kind of Culture would I like to be a part of? What are my colleagues doing, saying, thinking on a daily basis? How warm are they? How smart are they? How helpful? How friendly? What kind of language do they use - polite, casual, negative?

• Fill out the five parameters from the Adios Career Framework in detail in your journal. Write for a few days, go for regular Contemplation walks, think about what you wrote, write some more.

• If possible, go for a solitary Contemplation retreat all alone for 2-3 days.

• Use external information or guidance as necessary to make your decision and think about that in your Contemplation session.

• For this discussion between you and yourself to become deeper, you need to master two things - Silence and Contemplation.

All the best.

∽

ABOUT THE AUTHOR

Tarun Gulati is the founder of Adios, a mental fitness initiative that enables you to live a fulfilling, purposeful and peaceful life. It does that by training you in a regular habit of Contemplation - systematic deep thinking and self-reflection - on certain Adios principles that help you think more clearly, so you can make better decisions which lead to a more fulfilling and peaceful life.

He was naturally drawn to moments of self-reflection from a young age. He started capturing his thoughts in a notebook for a few years, marking the inception of what would become Adios later on. After working for a couple of international companies (Price Waterhouse, Mars), he started advising companies on certain strategic matters and playing the drums as a hobbyist. His own self-knowledge and Contemplation journey continued alongside these professional endeavors.

He created the Dot Movement, a weekend group initiative to enable people to pursue their hobbies in a non-judgmental manner. People used to meet over the weekend to encourage each other to sing, dance, write, go for a walk, etc. He conducted his first Adios Contemplation workshop in 2015 for the participants of the Dot Movement. He formally created the Adios Contemplation framework in 2020 and started training people in 2021. Since then, he has trained multiple people in the US and India, including startup founders, senior CXOs, actors, athletes, students, addicts, wellness and life coaches, therapists, homemakers and many others.

He also created an Adios framework to enable businesses to be created on a foundation of Contemplation on Values, Vision and Culture (www.FounderDecelerator.com) and Venus - an Adios framework for dating and relationships that emphasizes on finding yourself first before you find a partner (www.LoveIs-Venus.com). He has also created other sub-frameworks for a few other domains (choosing a career, stock market investing) and is in the process of creating more.

The Adios Contemplation framework is available as a systematic program on the mobile and web app plus monthly online group coaching sessions on www.adiosworld.com.

Contemplation on the Adios principles will help you create and maintain a deep connection with yourself, so you can think more clearly, so you can make personal and professional decisions that are right for you, which will lead to a more fulfilling, purposeful and peaceful life.

Contemplation empowers you to make all your decisions on your own, without depending excessively on anyone else, forever.

Made in the USA
Columbia, SC
03 May 2025

57497452R00143